Economic Growth Among Industrialized Countries:

Why the United States Lags

BY ROBERT M. DUNN, JR.

Assisted by SALIH N. NEFTCI

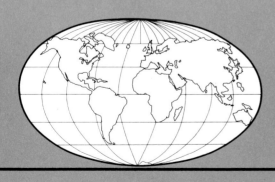

NPA Committee on
Changing International Realities

NPA's Committee on Changing International Realities and Their Implications for U.S. Policy

Profound changes have been taking place during the 1970s in the nature of the international political and economic system and in the position of the United States within it. These continuing developments involve new and highly complex kinds of interactions among nations. In consequence, many of the assumptions about international economic and political relationships that were relevant during the 1950s and '60s can no longer serve as valid bases for governmental and private policy making. Today and for the future, policy makers need new concepts and data relevant to the changing realities of the present period if they are to serve the interests of the United States and the welfare of the American people. And, because the United States has a predominantly private enterprise economy, policies affecting the ability of the U.S. private sector to function effectively both at home and abroad are of crucial importance for realizing these national goals.

Accordingly, in 1975, NPA established the Committee on Changing International Realities and Their Implications for U.S. Policy (CIR) to undertake a continuing two-part program. It consists of (1) research on the nature and probable future development of the new international realities and of U.S. capabilities and needs relative to them, and (2) based on these analyses and forecasts, suggestions for governmental and private policies to improve the international performance of the U.S. economy so that it can better protect and advance the interests of the United States and the well-being of the American people.

In accordance with NPA's practice, the CIR consists of experienced leaders from the main private-sector groups: business corporations and banks, labor unions, farm organizations, and the professions. The Committee meets twice a year to discuss subjects to be researched, to review outlines and drafts of studies under way and to consider their policy implications. Detailed guidance of the CIR's research program is carried on by subcommittees concerned with various subject areas. Professional and administrative staff services are provided to the Committee under the supervision of the Director of NPA's International Division.

For information about the CIR or NPA's other international committee and research activities, please get in touch with:

Neil J. McMullen
NPA Vice President and
Director, International Division

National Planning Association
1606 New Hampshire Avenue, N.W.
Washington, D.C. 20009
(202) 265–7685

A description of NPA as a whole and a list of its Officers and Board of Trustees are printed at the end of this publication.

Economic Growth Among Industrialized Countries:

Why the United States Lags

BY ROBERT M. DUNN, JR.
George Washington University

Assisted by SALIH N. NEFTCI
George Washington University

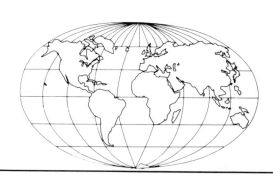

NPA Committee on
Changing International Realities

89

81 6293 6

**Economic Growth Among Industrialized
Countries: Why the United States Lags**

CIR Report #7
NPA Report #179

Price $5.50

ISBN 0-89068-053-1
Library of Congress
Catalog Card Number 80-81478

Copyright May 1980
by the
NATIONAL PLANNING ASSOCIATION
A voluntary association incorporated under the laws of
the District of Columbia
1606 New Hampshire Avenue, N.W.
Washington, D.C. 20009

Contents

Economic Growth Among Industrialized Countries:
Why the United States Lags

by Robert M. Dunn, Jr.
assisted by Salih N. Neftci

TABLES

A Statement by the Committee on Changing International Realities

Since its establishment, the primary concern of the Committee on Changing International Realities has been the international and domestic factors affecting the competitive position of the United States and implications of adverse changes in U.S. international competitiveness for domestic employment opportunities and the general well-being of the American people. In recent years, there has been increasing concern about both the growth performance and the international competitiveness of the U.S. economy. Today, the U.S. economy is at a crossroads. Policy makers are under considerable pressure to provide new directions so that the economy may continue to grow and Americans may once again enjoy economic security and improvements in their living standards.

Although the economy achieved a substantial rate of GNP growth during the recent cyclical recovery, this expansion was in large part generated by abnormally high rates of labor-force and employment growth—a phenomenon resulting from increasing female participation and the entry of the postwar "baby-boom" generation in the labor force. In contrast, productivity growth rates have been close to zero since 1973. This is particularly distressing given the slowing in labor-force growth expected for the balance of the century. If the economy is to maintain growth rates adequate to provide attractive employment opportunities, moderately rising real incomes for the working-age population, and a modest, but dignified, standard of living for the increasing numbers of retired and elderly people, then productivity growth will have to advance vigorously and the discouraging trends of the past decade will have to be reversed in the years ahead.

Progress on the productivity front will require economic policies that are premised on a sophisticated understanding of the complex determinants of the economy's capacity to utilize resources and produce goods efficiently. Equally important will be the formulation and implementation of policies that provide private citizens and businessmen with incentives and an environment of confidence about the future that encourage working, saving and investing to expand productive capacity and maintain the growth of rewarding employment opportunities.

In the interests of improving understanding and broadening areas of consensus, which are essential to the adoption of forward-looking policies, the Committee on Changing International Realities commissioned Dr. Robert Dunn, Jr. (assisted by Salih Neftci), of George Washington University, to undertake a study reviewing recent economic growth in the United States and comparing it with the growth rates of six other major industrial countries.

The authors conclude that inadequate levels of savings and investment—in both plant and equipment and research and development activity—are among the major impediments to U.S. productivity growth. After examining aspects of U.S. tax and regulatory policies that have contributed to the present situation, they propose changes that could help increase savings and investment and promote more rapid economic progress. They recommend a stabilization of regulatory policies and the establishment of long-term energy policies to reduce the uncertainty that inhibits investors.

We believe that, at this crucial juncture in American economic history, a reevaluation of U.S. domestic and international economic policies and the interrelationships between them is needed. The data and analysis provided by Dr. Dunn should make a substantial contribution to this effort and are worthy of the serious attention of private-sector groups, government policy makers and opinion leaders. Accordingly, regardless of whether we agree or disagree with all of the study's specific interpretations and conclusions, we believe that Dr. Dunn's study raises many important issues, provides valuable data and analyses, formulates policies deserving serious consideration, and will make an important contribution to resolving the economic problems confronting the nation. We are, therefore, pleased to recommend that it be published by NPA as a report signed by its authors.

Footnotes to the Statement

The study is well done, raises many important issues and should be published. However, I cannot support all the comments relating to energy and more particularly the concept of a "windfall profits tax." The tax currently being considered by Congress is actually an excise tax and imposes heavy taxes on increased oil production. — **Leroy Culbertson**   *(see page 61 of text)*

Any tax on domestic crude oil would reduce production incentives from their free market level, and would thus reduce economic efficiency. If a "light" tax is good, no tax is better. In this regard, the recently enacted "windfall profits tax" will reduce domestic petroleum production by about 1.5 million barrels per day. — **James E. Lee**   *(see page 61 of text)*

The recommendations to encourage research and development should be broadened to include a direct tax credit for R&D spending. R&D is the catalyst that makes step-function productivity gains possible. According to Professor Kendrick of George Washington University, roughly two-thirds of all advances in managerial and technological knowledge (which, in turn, accounted for roughly half of the U.S. increases in productivity between 1948-78) stem from formal programs that increase the stock of R&D. Texas Instruments' experience has confirmed that money invested in R&D is highly leveraged in its beneficial effect on productivity.

Texas Instruments Incorporated sponsored a study, prepared by Andrew Brimmer in cooperation with Data Resources, Inc., which demonstrates the positive impact of alternative R&D tax credits (10 percent, 25 percent and 50 percent) on industrial R&D expenditures, productivity and real GNP growth.

For example, the enactment in 1966 of a continuing 25 percent tax credit on industrial R&D expenditures would have added 0.2 percentage points to annual productivity gains during 1966-77, 0.3 percentage points per year in 1978-87, and 0.4 percentage points per year in 1988-97. To put these numbers in perspective, we only need to recall that the total productivity change in each of the four quarters of 1979 was actually negative. This 25 percent tax credit would, moreover, generate, for comparable time periods, average annual gains (in 1972 dollars) of about $2 billion, $5 billion and $11 billion in R&D expenditures; and approximately $4 billion, $36 billion and $102 billion in GNP.

Finally, we estimated that the tax cost of this program would average a net loss of $2.3 billion annually for the first 10 years. In subsequent time periods, however, the cumulative impact of R&D would begin to pay large
(Continued)

Footnotes Continued

dividends. Faster economic growth would produce larger tax gains and the net tax impact would become a positive $6.1 billion per year in the second decade, offsetting by roughly a 3-to-1 margin the tax losses in the previous period. These results indicate that the R&D tax credit is an investment that would yield significant positive returns to society as well as to private firms—**Mark Shepherd, Jr.** *(see pages 62–63 of text)*

Given the magnitude and complexity of Professor Dunn's task, explaining the recent poor economic performance of the U.S. relative to other industrial countries, it is not surprising that at least one of us would find fault with certain aspects of the completed study. I am concerned that because the study lacks a coherent theoretical framework, some of its conclusions and policy prescriptions do not follow from the analysis. Nevertheless, this study has identified many important issues and should serve to stimulate further discussion of how to provide an environment conducive to economic growth. —**Mark H. Willes**

Members of the Committee on Changing International Realities Signing the Statement

G.A. COSTANZO
Chairman; Vice Chairman, Citibank

GLENN E. WATTS
Vice Chairman; President, Communications Workers of America

WILLIAM R. PEARCE
Chairman of the Executive Committee; Corporate Vice President, Cargill Incorporated

ARTHUR J.R. SMITH
Secretary; President, National Planning Association

MARION H. ANTONINI
Group Vice President, Xerox Corporation

LEE S. APPLETON
Regional Vice President-East, Allis-Chalmers Corporation

ROBERT A. BELANGER
Senior Vice President, Bank of America

HOWARD W. BELL
Director & Financial Vice President, Standard Oil Company of California

RICHARD M. BISSELL, JR.
Consultant, The Exchange

JOHN C. BROOMAN
President & Chief Operating Officer, The Black & Decker Manufacturing Company

J.G. CLARKE
Director & Senior Vice President, Exxon Corporation

HENRY J. CLAYCAMP
Vice President, Corporate Planning, International Harvester Company

JACK H. CORNELY
President, Firestone International Company

*LEROY CULBERTSON
Senior Vice President of Corporate Planning & Budgeting, Phillips Petroleum Company

ALEXANDER A. CUNNINGHAM
President, General Motors Overseas Corporation

ROBERT B. DELANO
President, American Farm Bureau Federation

DONALD J. DONAHUE
Vice Chairman, Operations Officer, The Continental Group, Inc.

GEORGE T. FARRELL
Vice President, Mellon Bank N.A.

MURRAY H. FINLEY
President, Amalgamated Clothing & Textile Workers' Union

RAYMOND G. FISHER
Business Consultant, Greenwich, Connecticut

ROBERT R. FREDERICK
Executive Vice President & Sector Executive of International Sector, General Electric Company

RALPH W. GOLBY
Vice President, Schering-Plough Corporation

RICHARD J. GOODMAN
Vice President–Investor Relations, Continental Grain Company

WILLIAM W. GRANGER, JR.
Executive Vice President & President, International Foods Division, Beatrice Foods Company

ALLAN GRANT
Visalia, California

ROGER W. GRAY
Professor & Economist, Food Research Institute

ROBERT A. HANSON
President, Deere & Company

JOHN M. HENNESSY
Executive Vice President, The First Boston Corporation

G. GRIFFITH JOHNSON
Executive Vice President, Motion Picture Association of America, Inc.

LEONARD KAMSKY
Corporate Vice President, Business Planning & Economics Group, W.R. Grace & Company

ALONZO B. KIGHT
Vice President, International, Rockwell International

TOM KILLEFER
Chairman of the Board & Chief Executive Officer, United States Trust Company of New York

PETER F. KROGH
Dean, Edmund A. Walsh School of Foreign Service, Georgetown University

*JAMES E. LEE
President, Gulf Oil Corporation

EDWARD LITTLEJOHN
Vice President-Public Affairs, Pfizer, Inc.

*See footnotes to the Statement.

The opinions expressed and the recommendations presented in the Committee Statement are solely those of the individual members of the Committee on Changing International Realities whose signatures are offered hereto and do not represent the views of the National Planning Association or its staff. Committee members' agreement or disagreement with specific points of this Statement is expressed in signed footnotes.

*See footnotes to the Statement.

Introduction: Recent Economic Growth 1

In recent years, Americans have become increasingly dissatisfied with the performance of their economy. A broad feeling has developed that the postwar era of relatively rapid growth is over and that difficult times lie ahead. In the early and mid-1960s, most economists, government officials and many in the business community shared the optimistic view that the economy could be "managed" in a manner which would produce steady and fairly rapid economic growth without serious inflation. Warnings by some economists that popular demand-management policies would fail to produce such happy results beyond the short run were largely ignored.

The last half of the 1960s and the 1970s have been a great disappointment. Economic growth has been considerably less rapid than had been expected, and the economy has been plagued by combinations of inflation and unemployment far worse than anyone thought possible. Faith in the effectiveness of government macroeconomic policies has declined as a result of this experience, and doubts are now widely expressed about whether any set of fiscal and monetary policies could return the U.S. economy to the pattern of the mid-1960s.

The macroeconomic model which has been used to determine government policies since 1960 is entirely demand oriented. Policies have been designed to manage the level of aggregate demand in the economy with the goal of approximately matching the assumed steady growth of the economy's productive capacity. The supply side of the economy has been simply ignored under the assumption that the labor force and the stock of capital would grow at unchanging rates and that technology would advance as usual. If the productive capacity of the economy grows steadily at 3.5 to 4.0 percent, policy makers simply target aggregate demand at the known capacity figure.

The experience of the period since 1965 has raised serious doubts about this approach. There is an increasing appreciation that the capacity of the economy to produce does not automatically grow at a steady rate and that a variety of government policies may affect its growth. Macroeconomic models which ignore supply-side considerations are increasingly understood to be seriously flawed, if not almost useless.

Classical economists such as Adam Smith and David Ricardo argued long ago that the performance of an economy was determined primarily by the supply side, but this point was largely ignored by John Maynard Keynes.[1] As disappointment with the performance of the U.S. economy has become more general (if not universal), economists have lost a great deal of their confidence in the previously accepted Keynesian macroeconomic model and in its implicit assumptions. Conventional Keynesian wisdom of the mid-1960s was attacked first by the monetarists and

---

1   John M. Keynes, *The General Theory of Employment, Interest and Money* (London: McMillan and Co., 1936).

more recently by the rational expectations school led by Robert Lucas.[2] Macroeconomic theory is in a period of transition as purely demand-oriented models are replaced by approaches which attempt to include both demand-management and supply-side effects. The relationship between demand-management policies and changes in the capacity of the economy to produce is, however, complicated and only dimly perceived. As a result, macroeconomists as a group are now considerably less certain in their understanding of the economy than was the case a few years ago. The worsening performance of the economy has been paralleled by the declining predictive performance of macroeconomic models, and the result is the current controversy and conflict within academic macroeconomics.

Although there is currently no clear consensus in the area of macroeconomic theory, there is a widespread feeling among economists that the failures of the post-1965 period are in large part attributable to supply-side problems. The purpose of this study is to analyze the performance of the U.S. economy during recent years with particular emphasis on factors which affect its capacity to produce. This analysis will be based in part on comparisons between the U.S. economy and those of other major OECD countries in order to attempt to identify factors which determine how well the United States has done relative to its major competitors. This will be particularly important in the area of government policies, where it may be possible to suggest what kind of public policies have encouraged or discouraged relatively rapid growth in the productive capacities of various OECD economies.

A word of warning may be appropriate here. The following pages represent a brief treatment of very complex phenomena. The treatment is based on existing work in economics, but many of the problems which are discussed remain unresolved and others are only vaguely understood. The present discussion cannot "solve" all these problems or suggest totally original solutions, but it attempts to illuminate problems and to suggest some possible policy options. More complete answers will hopefully result from professional research in the years ahead.

MEASUREMENT OF MACROECONOMIC PERFORMANCE

One initial problem is how to define and measure the "performance" of an economy. There are a large number of statistical series which measure one aspect or another of the economy's behavior and, in a study of this length, it is not possible to deal with all or even most of them. This exercise will focus primarily on the key indicators of the supply side of macroeconomic performance: increases in real GNP per capita and growth rates of labor productivity.

Although growth of real GNP per capita is the most common indicator of an economy's performance, this and other related statistics have some sizable flaws as measures of broad economic welfare. GNP does not, for example, include any allowances for increases in leisure. If the average work week declines as people choose to use increases in labor productivity to buy more leisure rather than more

---

2   Milton Friedman's 1968 paper, "The Role of Monetary Policy" (*American Economic Review*), is a classic attack by the monetarists. The more recent criticism of the rational expectations school is summarized in "After Keynesian Macroeconomics" by Robert E. Lucas and Thomas Sargent, published by the Federal Reserve Bank of Boston in 1978.

goods and services, economic welfare has clearly improved but GNP data will not reflect that improvement.

Economic welfare may also be affected by how the income derived from a country's output is distributed. Voters in the United States and elsewhere have indicated a fairly strong preference for some degree of income redistribution through a progressive income tax and transfer payments. This suggests that publicly perceived economic welfare is improved by such redistribution policies, but GNP figures do not reflect this aspect of economic well-being. GNP data would not be affected by a redistribution of income from the poor to the rich or vice versa. Society has a variety of economic welfare goals other than GNP per capita, and improvements in these areas are not reflected in the data used in this study.

GNP figures also misrepresent real economic output because no allowance is made in the data for externalities, such as air and water pollution. When such pollution was unregulated, it represented a real cost of producing various goods that was not reflected in the cost figures of the polluting industries or in economic statistics for the economy as a whole. As a result, real output and economic welfare were overstated by published GNP figures. As environmental protection laws are passed and clean-up efforts are begun, these unmeasured costs decline and the published GNP figures become more accurate. Since previous GNP data overstated real output because of the lack of allowance for pollution costs, and since current GNP data more accurately reflect real output because pollution has been reduced, published GNP figures will imply less rapid economic growth between the two periods than actually occurred. Properly measured output increased when air and water pollution were reduced, but published output data does not include this increase. The same problem exists in the areas of consumer product safety and occupational safety and health. To the extent that these regulatory efforts improve real economic welfare, GNP figures understate economic growth.

Output and resulting income that are not recorded in tax returns are another source of error in the GNP data. There is reason to believe that high marginal income taxes have encouraged the growth of a large "off-the-books" sector of the economy in which output is produced and incomes are received, but no taxes are paid. Since GNP data come in large part from tax returns, the growth of such an "underground" or "hidden economy" results in GNP figures that underestimate how rapidly the economy is actually growing. Transactions in this sector of the economy are typically carried on in currency, and the rapidly growing demand for currency in the United States suggests that such activity is increasing. Perfectly legal do-it-yourself activities, which are strongly encouraged by high marginal income tax rates, have the same effect. Many such activities do not show up in recorded GNP data and, if they are of growing importance, the result is that GNP figures understate economic growth.

GNP levels in different countries can be compared only through exchange rates, and this creates another problem. If market exchange rates accurately reflect the relative purchasing powers of currencies, the use of current market exchange rates to make international GNP comparisons will produce accurate results. If, however, an exchange rate misrepresents the relative purchasing power of two currencies, its use in comparing GNP levels will produce misleading results. Frequently published figures indicating that Swedish GNP per capita is higher than that in the United States, for example, result from the fact that the Swedish Krona has been badly overvalued. The recent devaluations of the Krona produce somewhat more realistic results, but Swedish GNP per capita is probably still overstated when translated into dollars at current exchange rates. The use of market exchange rates produces a particularly large problem when these rates change rapidly. A 10 percent appreciation of the Deutschemark, for example, will produce the appearance of a 10 percent growth in German GNP when measured in U.S. dollars. No such growth occurred, but either the previous or the latter exchange rate misrepresented the relative purchasing power of the two currencies. Attempts will be made in this study to use exchange rates that have been adjusted to approximate actual relative purchasing powers, but such adjustments are far from precise or fully dependable.

Labor productivity figures for the economy as a whole are typically presented in the form of GNP per employee, which is also a less than perfect measure of economic performance. GNP per worker fails to deal with the problem of measuring output in the services and government sectors. The quality of a privately provided service may improve or deteriorate without being fully reflected in GNP and hence in labor productivity data. Since there is no market price for government services, their value is simply entered in GNP at cost. As a result, labor productivity may improve or deteriorate in the government sector without such a change being reflected in GNP per employee.

Despite this rather long list of problems with published GNP and labor productivity figures as measures of a nation's economic performance, they will be used as the principal indicators in this study. The first reason for doing so is that

TABLE 1-1. REAL GNP PER CAPITA: AVERAGE ANNUAL RATES OF CHANGE

	1960–65	1965–71	1971–79
U.S.	3.2%	1.5%	2.4%
Canada	3.7	3.3	2.8
France	4.4	4.5	3.0
Italy	4.5	4.5	2.4
Japan	9.0	10.0	4.4
U.K.	2.5	2.1	1.8
West Germany	3.8	3.7	2.9
Average	4.4	4.2	2.8
Average, excluding the U.S.	4.7	4.7	2.9

Sources: OECD, *National Accounts* (1952–77), and OECD, *Economic Outlook* (December 1979), p. 13; 1979 data based on OECD forecasts; Wilson Pritchett III, *World Population Estimates, 1978* (Washington, D.C.: The Environmental Fund, 1978). 1979 estimates of real GNP per capita growth assume a continuation of 1978 population growth rates.

these indicators of output, unlike broader and more general concepts of economic welfare, are measurable and are available in a comparable form for a number of relevant countries. Attempts have been made to develop "social indicators" which measure an economy's social and economic welfare in a broad sense, but these efforts have had limited success. For the moment, GNP data constitute the broadest available measure of an economy's performance.

Real GNP per capita does represent a large part of economic welfare in the sense that, if real output is growing rapidly, a society has the option of using newly available resources to deal with a variety of distributional and broad welfare problems. It is much easier to change relative income shares and provide for growing public needs when real output per capita is increasing than when such growth is lacking. GNP per capita may not be synonymous with economic welfare, but growth in that measure of output makes it possible for society to deal with broader welfare issues in a democratic context. Finally, GNP per capita and labor productivity figures receive a great deal of public and political attention, and are widely seen as indicators of how well an economy is doing. Governments that preside over economies which do badly in terms of these measures have a great deal to explain if they expect to remain in power. Whatever their drawbacks, the growth of GNP per capita and labor productivity are politically accepted measures of national economic performance that command a great deal of attention in political debates and in broader discussions of economic problems.

RECENT HISTORY: THE UNITED STATES
AND ITS MAJOR COMPETITORS

Table 1-1 compares the rate of growth of U.S. GNP per capita with those of a number of other major industrial countries during the period since 1960. These countries—Canada, West Germany, France, the United Kingdom, Italy, and Japan—will be used for comparative purposes throughout this study. Two broad conclusions emerge from the table. First, the United States did relatively poorly through the 1960s and during the beginning of the 1970s. U.S. economic growth ranked next to last in 1960-65 and was last in the following five years. Growth rates in the other OECD countries averaged 4.7 percent in 1960-65 compared to 3.2 percent for the United States. In the next six years, the average for the others again was 4.7 percent, while U.S. growth fell to an average rate of only 1.5 percent. Second, in the 1971-79 period, the pattern changed. Growth rates declined significantly in the other OECD countries but increased modestly in the United States. For this period, the U.S. growth rate was not far behind the average for the other six countries. Thus, during the 1960s, growth in the other major OECD countries was quite rapid, and the United States lagged badly, particularly late in the decade. In the 1970s, everybody did badly, but relative to the others the United States did not do quite as poorly as it had earlier.

This pattern of comparisons depends in part on the choice of years which divide the periods. These countries did not follow the same cyclical patterns during this 17-year period, so any divisions into subperiods are certain to produce problems in comparing performance across countries. The United States was in a strong cyclical recovery in 1976-79, for example, while the other OECD countries as a group had a recovery which lagged behind the U.S. pattern by over a year.[3] As a result, 1979 U.S. output would be closer to full capacity and a likely cyclical peak than was the case for the other countries. This difference in the cyclical patterns of these countries means that the relative performance of the United States looks somewhat better than it should for the 1971–79 period. The United States entered the 1974–75 recession faster and, consequently, approached full capacity output levels well ahead of the other industrial countries.

These differences in growth rates produce an interesting pattern of GNP per capita levels for the various countries. In Table 1–2, U.S. GNP per capita is set at 100 for each of the recorded years and the GNP per capita in the other countries is measured as a percentage of the U.S. level. These comparisons are made at current market exchange rates.

As can be seen in this table, differences between per capita GNP in the United States and elsewhere narrowed considerably from 1950–75. Canada completely caught up, and France and Germany came very close. Using this measure, the narrowing continued in the early 1970s. The main problem with this table is that it uses current market exchange rates, which probably do not represent the true relative purchasing powers of the currencies for a complete range of goods and services produced by the various countries. An attempt was made to adjust the data in the previous table to eliminate this distortion, and Table 1–3 shows the resulting indices of per capita GNP.

The figures in Table 1–3 are an approximation of relative per capita GNP levels at exchange rates which more accurately represent the true relative purchasing powers of the various currencies. As can be seen in this table, the tendency for differences between U.S. and other OECD GNP per capita levels to narrow remains clear, but the extent of the narrowing is not as striking as was the case when market

TABLE 1-2. COMPARISONS OF PER CAPITA OUTPUT
US = 100 (Using Market Rates of Exchange)

	1950	1960	1970	1975
U.S.	100	100	100	100
Canada	66	79	80	100
France	37	48	58	89
Italy	16	25	36	44
Japan	NA	16	39	62
U.K.	38	49	46	57
West Germany	25	46	64	95

Source: "Comparing Per Capita Output Internationally," by Jai-Hoon Yang, Federal Reserve Bank of St. Louis, *Review* (May 1978).

---

3   The slow recovery of the European economies may also be structural rather than purely cyclical in nature. Because of their almost complete dependence on imported oil (except the United Kingdom), the European economies have had to adjust even more than the United States to the oil shocks of the 1970s.

TABLE 1-3. COMPARISONS OF PER CAPITA OUTPUT
US = 100 (Using "Adjusted" Exchange Rates)

	1950	1960	1970	1975
U.S.	100	100	100	100
Canada	75	77	83	93
France	46	58	75	71
Italy	25	33	46	46
Japan	NA	NA	62	71
U.K.	55	64	60	61
West Germany	36	64	75	76

Source: See Table 1-2.

exchange rates were used. This means that the U.S. dollar depreciated faster than relative rates of inflation would warrant during the early 1970s.

Despite the change introduced by the use of more realistic exchange rates, it remains clear that the other OECD countries grew faster than the United States and closed the gap between their GNP per capita levels and those prevailing in the United States during the 1950–75 period. This pattern was evident in both the 1950s and '60s. In the early 1970s, however, the pattern was less clear. The slowing of growth in the rest of the OECD countries reduced the rate at which these countries as a group gained on the United States. Canada and Japan continued to grow considerably more rapidly than the United States during the early 1970s, and only France grew more slowly.

A recent study by Kravis, Heston and Summers contains a quite thorough attempt to compare per capita output and income levels based on realistic exchange rates for a number of countries, but unfortunately it deals with only a brief time period. It suggests that during the first half of the 1970s, Japan, France and Germany grew more rapidly than the United States and that the United Kingdom and Italy grew slightly less rapidly. Canada was not included in the Kravis study.[4] The minor differences between the conclusions of the Yang study and the

[4]

Indexes of Real GDP per Capita in International Dollars
United States = 100

	1967	1970	1973	1974	1975
France	NA	73.2	76.1	78.6	79.5
Italy	NA	49.2	47.0	47.7	47.1
Japan	48.3	59.2	64.0	63.2	65.1
United Kingdom	61.9	63.5	60.6	60.5	62.0
West Germany	NA	78.2	77.4	78.9	79.2

Irving Kravis, Alan Heston and Robert Summers, *International Comparisons of Real Product and Purchasing Power* (Baltimore: published for the World Bank by the Johns Hopkins University Press, 1978), p. 14.

Kravis volume may be because the latter effort used gross domestic product rather than GNP as the measure of output. The two concepts differ in their treatment of net dividend and interest flows in the balance of payments.

LABOR PRODUCTIVITY: A SIMILAR PATTERN, BUT WORSE

U.S. labor productivity growth, which is the source of increases in output per capita whenever labor-force participation rates and the length of the average work week are constant, has been unimpressive for some time and has recently become much worse (see Table 1–4).

During the 1950–70 period, U.S. labor productivity growth was the slowest of the countries studied here—less than half as fast as those of Germany, Italy and Japan. In the following seven years, labor productivity growth declined significantly in every country except France, where a slight increase occurred. In the 1970–77 period, U.S. productivity growth tied for last, and again was less than half as rapid as the rates of Germany, France, Italy, and Japan.

The recent decline in labor productivity growth among the major OECD countries becomes even more striking if the 1973–79 period is used and is compared with 1963–73, as Table 1–5 demonstrates. Labor productivity growth fell sharply in all of the listed countries, and in the United States there was virtually no growth at all. During a period of six years, U.S. labor productivity grew by a total of about 0.5 percent. Other countries experienced slowdowns, with the Japanese, British and Italian declines particularly striking, but they at least had some growth. The most recent figures suggest negative U.S. labor productivity growth for 1979.

Two broad conclusions emerge from the data. First, all of the major OECD countries experienced a period of rapid labor productivity growth in the 1950s and '60s, which slowed dramatically in the 1970s. Second, U.S. labor productivity growth was considerably less impressive than that prevailing in the other industrialized market economies during the 1950s and 1960s, was worse throughout the 1970s, and

TABLE 1-4. AVERAGE ANNUAL CHANGES IN LABOR
PRODUCTIVITY
(GDP per Manhour)

	1870–1913	1913–50	1950–70	1970–77
U.S.	2.1%	2.5%	2.5%	2.0%
Canada	2.0	2.3	2.9	2.2
France	1.8	1.7	4.8	5.1
Italy	1.2	1.8	5.4	5.0
Japan	1.8	1.4	7.9	5.7
U.K.	1.1	1.5	2.8	2.4
West Germany	1.9	1.2	6.2	4.7

Source: "Long-Run Dynamics of Productivity Growth," A. Maddison, *Banco Nazionale Del Lavoro Quarterly Review* (March 1979).

TABLE 1-5. AVERAGE ANNUAL CHANGES IN LABOR
            PRODUCTIVITY
            (GNP per Employee)

	1963–73	1973–79	Difference
U.S.	1.9%	0.1%	− 1.8%
Canada	2.4	0.4	− 2.0
France	4.6	2.7	− 1.9
Italy	5.4	1.5	− 3.9
Japan	8.7	3.3	− 5.4
U.K.	3.0	0.4	− 2.6
West Germany	4.6	3.1	− 1.5

Source: OECD, *Economic Outlook* (July 1979), p. 26, and (December 1979), p. 25; 1979 data based on OECD forecasts.

appalling during the last few years. Since 1975, labor productivity growth has slowed sharply in the industrialized countries and has almost stopped in the United States.

There is an interesting paradox in the comparison between U.S. GNP and U.S. labor productivity growth in the 1970s. Real GNP growth continued and increased slightly in years in which labor productivity growth was declining sharply. There is no such pattern in the rest of the industrialized countries, where GNP and labor productivity data followed similar patterns.

The dominant reason for the paradox in the U.S. data can be found in the rate of growth in the U.S. labor force. Between 1970 and 1976, the U.S. civilian labor force grew by about 13 percent, or by over 2 percent a year. With the exception of Canada, where labor-force growth was even more rapid, the other industrialized countries had very slow labor-force growth, and the German labor force actually fell by 2.5 percent during this period. Japan, France, Italy, and the United Kingdom all experienced labor-force growth of less than 1 percent a year. Between 1976 and 1978, the U.S. labor force grew by about 6 percent, or at a rate of 3 percent a year, which represents a further acceleration.

This extremely rapid growth is not the result of a parallel increase in the U.S. population. Between 1970 and 1978, the population grew by only 6.7 percent, which means an annual rate of considerably less than 1 percent. In contrast, the labor force grew by over 21 percent during this eight-year period, as the percentage of the U.S. population in the labor force rose dramatically. The civilian participation rate in 1970 was 40.4 percent; by 1979, it had increased to 45.9 percent, meaning that an additional 5.5 percent of the population joined the civilian labor force during this period.

The increase in the U.S. participation rate had three dominant causes, none of which will continue through the 1980s. First, the U.S. armed forces were reduced by 1.4 million, or about 1.6 percent of the total labor force. The second was a huge increase in the participation rate of women, which has almost approached that of men but is unlikely to rise much more.

The third and most important source of labor-force growth has been the arrival of the postwar baby boom at working age. During the 1950s, the U.S. working-age (20–64) population grew by only about 6 million, or at a rate of 0.6 million per year. This growth accelerated to 1.3 million per year during the 1960s and to 1.9 million per year from 1970 through 1978.[5] The growth of this age population will continue at about 1.9 million per year until 1985 as the last part of the baby boom enters the labor force, but the sharp decline in the U.S. birth rate during the latter half of the 1960s means that this growth will slow sharply during succeeding years. The growth of the working-age population is now projected to average only 1.2 million per year during the 1985–90 period and then decline to only 1.0 million per year during the 1990s. The age distribution of the U.S. population means that labor-force growth accelerated rapidly in the 1960s and '70s, that it will maintain its recent rate for five more years, and that it will decline sharply for the remainder of the century.[6]

Unless an unexpectedly large number of Americans accept the option of working beyond age 65 which became legal in 1979, the number of retirees will increase sharply during the 1980s and '90s, significantly reducing the number of active workers per retiree and thereby increasing the relative costs of maintaining the social security system and other programs for the aged.[7]

U.S. real GNP continued to grow fairly rapidly in the mid-1970s because very low labor productivity growth was offset by an extraordinary increase in the labor-force participation rate. That increase is likely to be coming to an end, and the civilian labor force can be expected to increase much more slowly as the 1980s pass.

An end of the U.S. labor-force boom will mean that U.S. GNP per capita can grow only to the extent that labor productivity grows. It will no longer be possible to sustain fairly rapid output growth purely on the basis of a big increase in the number of Americans holding jobs. If U.S. labor productivity growth does not recover from the appalling experience of the mid-1970s, the United States can expect very little growth in real output per capita through the 1980s.

The following sections will analyze the major causes of the recent pattern of slow labor productivity and general economic growth in the United States and will suggest a set of policy changes which might be expected to improve the situation. Chapter 2 provides a brief introduction to the theory of economic growth, stressing in particular the role of savings and investment as a share of GNP in the growth process. Chapter 3 examines U.S. savings rates during recent years compared to those in other countries and suggests some likely reasons for low U.S. savings rates. Chapter 4 deals with investment, again comparing the U.S. experience to those of its major industrial competitors and indicating why U.S. investment in plant and equipment has been such a low percentage of GNP. Chapter 5 deals with research and development as sources of economic growth and with the impact of recent oil

---

5   *The Economic Report of the President, 1979,* p. 213.

6   *Communication from the Board of Trustees, Federal Old-Age and Survivors Insurance and Disability Insurance Trust Funds,* 95th Cong., 2nd sess., House Document No. 95-336, May 16, 1978, p. 57.

7   Ibid, p. 57.

price increases on U.S. terms of trade and hence on real incomes. Chapter 6 uses the analysis of the previous pages to suggest a set of policies which would encourage considerably faster productivity growth in the United States during the next decade. These options are far from painless and are not suggested with the expectation that they will be universally popular. They deserve discussion, however, if this country is serious about trying to reverse the recent pattern of slow growth, higher than desirable unemployment rates and generally poor economic performance.

Sources of Economic Growth: A Brief Introduction to Theory 2

Economic growth is both one of the most important areas in economics and one of the most complex and least understood. It is complex in the sense that virtually everything that goes on within an economy can affect growth prospects, and it is incompletely understood because of that complexity. Growth economics has become one of the most mathematical areas within economic theory, and is also an area in which the work of economic historians, sociologists and anthropologists is highly relevant.

Economic growth is incompletely understood in part because decisions to invest in plant and equipment are central to growth, and these decisions are based on a large number of factors, some of which are not measurable or even observable. Expectations, Keynes' "animal spirits," and business "confidence" are all vital to business investment decisions, but are very difficult to measure. Models of investments have been developed which are based solely on observable variables, but they miss a great deal and often have had poor predictive powers.

What follows cannot be a complete survey of the factors which determine an economy's rate of growth. This study will instead be based on a straightforward concept of output and growth determination that stresses a few of the more important variables. This approach is "supply" oriented in that it deals with factors which determine the capacity of the economy to produce output rather than with the level of aggregate demand for that output. This is done because of a presumption, noted in the previous chapter, that the recent lack of adequate economic growth in the United States and elsewhere is largely the result of a lack of growth in productive capacity, rather than of insufficient aggregate demand. The problem is no longer managing aggregate demand to catch up with full capacity employment, but one of aggregate demand which is inflationary because potential supply is growing so slowly.

The classical view of output determination is that an economy's capacity to produce is positively related to the size of its capital stock, its labor force, its productive land (including minerals under the land), and the state of technology. If, as is likely in the 1980s, a constant relationship between population and labor force (a constant participating rate) is assumed, output determination can then be simplified into the statement that output per capita is positively related to the size of the capital stock per worker, the amount of productive land per worker, and the state of technology.[1] This simplified approach assumes a closed economy, that is, the absence of international trade. If the economy is open, one more variable must be added: the country's terms of trade, i.e., the relationship between export prices

---

1   This assumes that the production function has constant returns to scale, that is, that the economy does not automatically become more efficient as it becomes larger.

and import prices. The real income which a country derives from a given amount of output is positively related to its terms of trade because that price ratio determines the quantity of imports that it can buy with revenue derived from a given amount of exports. If export prices rise sharply, for example, an unchanged volume of exports will pay for a larger bundle of imports and the country has a higher real income. The role of the terms of trade in determining a country's real income can be seen most clearly for a country such as Zaire which exports almost nothing but copper. When copper prices are high, Zaire enjoys a sharp increase in real income almost irrespective of whatever else happens in the economy. When copper prices are low, as they were during the mid-1970s, Zaire suffers as real income falls no matter what else happens.

The simplified classical model now suggests that output per capita is positively related to the capital/labor ratio, the land/labor ratio, the state of technology, and the country's terms of trade. The per capita rate of growth of productive capacity is then positively related to changes in the capital/labor ratio, changes in the land/labor ratio, improvements in technology, and increases in the country's terms of trade. The importance of the terms of trade depends on how deeply the economy is involved in international trade. If exports and imports are a large percentage of GNP, changes in the terms of trade become more important and vice versa.

Since a country's land mass is presumably fixed, the land to labor (and land to population) ratio must fall through time as the population and labor force grow. This necessary decline in the land/labor ratio discourages economic growth—which led many early classical economists (particularly Malthaus) to decidedly pessimistic conclusions. The history of modern industrial countries suggests that it is a negative factor which can be easily overcome by other forces if the population does not grow too rapidly and if technological progress is fairly rapid. The potential importance of the land/population ratio is clearer in the case of India, with a population of 650 million people that is growing at the rate of over 2 percent a year, and which has a rather small stock of highly productive land. The land/population ratio will not be dealt with further in this study, because low rates of population growth and rapid technological change in agriculture have meant that it is not a major problem for the advanced OECD countries, and because the stock of land is given so that there is nothing that a country could do about this restraint even if it were a problem.

For an economy like that of the United States where international trade has not been a major factor in GNP, the dominant factors in determining the rate of per capita economic growth become the rate of growth of the capital stock per worker and the rate of improvement in technology. Investment in plant and equipment that increases the capital stock is critically tied to technological advance through the fact that most new technology is embodied in new capital equipment. Technology becomes productive, not when it is invented, but when it is actually put to use, and that typically requires new capital. Very few new inventions or productive improvements can be used with old machinery or equipment. As a result, new machinery uses new technology and vice versa. This means that the level of technology actually being used in an economy is inversely related to the average age of its stock of machinery and equipment. If the capital stock is generally quite old, the economy will be based on old and/or obsolete technology, but if the capital stock is young, the country will be using newer and more productive techniques.

The average age of the capital stock depends on the current rate of investment in new plant and equipment and hence on the rate of growth of the capital stock. A high rate of investment in new plant and equipment and a resulting rapid growth of the capital stock mean a relatively young capital stock and vice versa. (The same argument holds for the population. A rapidly growing population will have a relatively low average age. Workers, unlike machines, are assumed to become more productive as they become older, so rapid population growth tends to lower the average productivity of the labor force.)

A high rate of investment in plant and equipment thus has positive effects on economic growth in two separate but equally important ways. First, such an investment increases the capital/labor ratio, which would increase output per worker even if technology were constant. Second, new investment typically embodies new technology, so a high rate of investment in plant and equipment means a relatively young capital stock that uses newer and more productive technology.[2] The importance of investment in new plant and equipment for labor productivity growth is suggested in Figure 2-1. The difference between Japan and the United States is particularly striking. Canada's rate of labor productivity growth is low for its rates of investment because of the very rapid labor-force growth it has experienced in recent years. This labor-force growth — caused in part by substantial immigration — requires high rates of investment just to maintain the capital/labor ratio.

---

2   The role of investment in plant and equipment as a major source of economic growth is a widely discussed topic in the academic literature on labor productivity. Most researchers working in this area have reached the unsurprising conclusion that the percentage of GNP invested in plant and equipment, or the rate of growth of the fixed capital stock, is a vital if not a dominant source of advancing labor productivity and hence of general economic growth. Edward Denison is an exception to this concensus: his work suggests that neither investment nor any other identifiable factors have caused the lag in U.S. productivity growth, and he is left with a sizable residual or unexplained part of the decline. His views have not found wide acceptance among students of the subject, most of whom have concluded that the low percentage of U.S. GNP which is invested in new plant and equipment (which uses new technology) has been a major source of the poor productivity performance which has plagued the U.S. economy. For Denison's views, see *Accounting for United States Economic Growth: 1929–69* (Washington, D.C.: Brookings Institution, 1974) and his more recent *Accounting for Slower Economic Growth: The United States in the 1970s* (Washington, D.C.: Brookings Institution, 1979). The dominant view that investment ratios are critical to understanding productivity growth can be found in a number of works by John Kendrick, including "Productivity Trends and the Recent Slowdown: Causal Factors and Policy Options" in William Fellner, ed., *Contemporary Economic Problems* (Washington, D.C.: American Enterprise Institute, 1979) and "The Contribution of Capital to Postwar Growth of Industrialized Countries" in *U.S. Economic Growth from 1976 to 1986: Prospects, Problems and Patterns, Vol. I, Productivity,* Joint Economic Committee, 94th Cong., 2nd sess., October 1976. Dale Jorgenson and Mieko Nishimizu reach similar conclusions in "U.S. and Japanese Economic Growth: An International Comparison," *Economic Journal,* Vol. 88 (December 1978), pp. 707–726. Their analysis stresses the role of *new* plant and equipment as embodying new and more productive technology. See also John R. Norsworthy and Michael Harper, "The Role of Capital Formation in the Recent Slowdown in Productivity Growth," *Working Paper #27,* U.S. Department of Labor, Bureau of Labor Statistics, Office of Productivity, January 1979. See also Michael McCarthy, "The U.S. Productivity Growth Recession: History and Prospects for the Future," *Journal of Finance* (June 1978), p. 977, for support of the view that low levels of investment in plant and equipment have been a central cause of slow growth. John R. Norsworthy, Michael Harper and Kent Kunze suggest in a more recent article that the 1965–73 slowdown in U.S. productivity growth cannot be easily explained by the behavior of investment, but that the further slowdown that occurred in 1973–78 is clearly attributable to less than adequate capital formation. See "The Slowdown in Productivity Growth: Analysis of Some Contributing Factors," *Brookings Papers on Economic Activity,* #2 (1979), pp. 384–421. Except for Denison there seems to be a concensus among researchers in the area that slow rates of productivity growth are in large part the result of rates of investment in new plant and equipment which are not adequate to increase significantly the capital/labor ratio or to maintain a relatively young and hence technologically current capital stock.

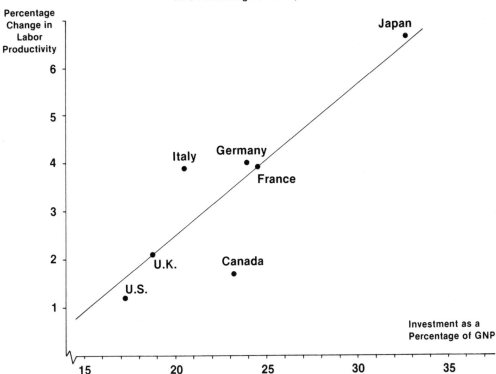

FIGURE 2-1. Percentage Changes in Labor Productivity Versus Investment as a Percentage of GNP, 1963–79*

*The following regression was used: percent change in productivity = -4.0295 + 0.32397(I/GNP); standard deviations of 1.78697 and 0.076735, respectively, and R² = 0.78.

Data source: Tables 1–5 and 4–1. Investment data only go through 1978.

Thus far, this discussion has followed the early view of economic growth in which capital consists only of physical plant and equipment. It has become clear in recent years that capital invested in education and training, widely known as human capital, is also important to economic growth. Labor productivity is obviously increased as workers become better educated or more thoroughly trained, and investment in education has been a significant source of economic growth in this and other economies. A great deal of human capital is created through on-the-job training. As the average age of the labor force increases, labor productivity rises. This should increase labor productivity in the United States during the next two decades as the baby-boom population ages. The remainder of this study, however, will not deal with human capital, both because accurate and current data on investment in education among countries is not readily available and because it does not appear that a lack of such investment has been a major problem in this or other major OECD economies.

THE SAVINGS/INVESTMENT RELATIONSHIP

An understanding of the behavior of investment as a source of capacity growth must begin with the point that, in a closed economy, investment is possible only to the extent that the economy as a whole saves. Since total incomes equal output, if the economy spends all of its income on current consumption (private plus public), then no output—that is, real resources—remains available for investment in plant and equipment. In the case of a closed economy, the rate of savings determines the availability of real resources for productive investment.

The savings/investment relationship becomes slightly more complicated when it is noted that both the private sector (households and businesses) and the public sector can save or "dissave." The savings rate which is relevant as a limit on investment is all private savings in households and businesses *plus* the public sector's operating surplus. More typically in modern industrial countries, it is private savings *minus* the public-sector deficit. The critical point here is that public-sector deficits necessitate a level of private investment that is less than the rate of private saving. Private savings can finance either productive investment or public-sector deficits. The simple Keynesian identity is:

$$I_p = S_p + (T - G)$$

where: I_p = private investment
S_p = private savings
T = public-sector tax revenues
G = government expenditures

It then follows that S_p can exceed I_p if G can exceed T.[3]

This identity assumes that the economy can absorb domestically (consume plus invest) only an amount of real resources equal to its current output. In other words, the rest of the world cannot be a source of net inflows of real resources. However, if it becomes possible for a country to run and finance a current-account deficit,[4] that restriction no longer holds and the economy can invest more than it saves. Similarly, a current-account surplus necessarily implies that the economy is investing less domestically than it saves. For the world as a whole, total saving still equals investment, so any excess of investment over saving via a current-account deficit in one country must be offset by an excess of saving over investment via a current-account surplus elsewhere.

The above identity now becomes:

$$I_p = S_p + (T-G) + (M-X)$$

where: M = imports of goods and services
X = exports of goods and services

It then follows that I_p can exceed $S_p + (T-G)$ if M can exceed X.

An economy which has a current-account deficit will invest domestically more than it saves and vice versa.

---

3   This statement is an identity *ex post*, but can be interpreted in an *ex ante* equilibrium condition.

4   The current account is the sum of all exports of goods and services minus the sum of all imports of goods and services. If the United States is in surplus, it is selling more abroad than it is buying from the rest of the world and vice versa. Outflows of funds for transfer payments (foreign aid) are viewed as analagous to a purchase of foreign goods for the purpose of constructing this balance.

The previous identity is always true regardless of how investment, savings or government deficits are determined. As a result, it cannot be used by itself to "explain" what "causes" changes in investment or savings. It can be used, however, to create a framework within which it is possible to discuss the behavior of the economy.

Interpreted in this way, a study of the process of economic growth begins by analyzing both sides of the equality, that is, why businesses decide to invest in new plant and equipment and, quite separately, why the economy saves, where saving (or dissaving) can be carried on by both the private and public sectors. In the United States and similar economies, the recent experience has been that the private sector saves and the public sector dissaves. An economy will grow rapidly if the business sector decides to invest a great deal in new plant and equipment *and* if the economy as a whole saves enough to make possible that level of investment. Low levels of savings or a lack of positive investment decisions by the business sector will produce low rates of economic growth.

If fiscal and monetary policies are managed to avoid clear cases of insufficient aggregate demand, as in the 1930s, differences between total savings provided by the economy and levels of investment intended by the business sector are reconciled primarily through changes in interest rates. If the economy saves less than the business sector wants to invest, the flow of funds into capital markets from savers will not be sufficient to meet the borrowing needs of those making plant and equipment investments. Interest rates will rise until marginal investments are discouraged due to excessive financing costs and increased savings are encouraged by more attractive interest rates. If the economy is saving more than businesses want to invest, an excess supply of "loanable funds" will lower interest rates, with the opposite effects.[5]

---

5   Since there are several regulations and laws which affect interest rates, this function may not be performed instantaneously through the movement of rates. Interest rates are not determined solely through the above mentioned equality. Interest rate determinations are complex and are an economywide phenomena.

Savings Rates: The U.S. Experience **3**

The previous chapter suggested that an economy's ability to invest in new plant and equipment, and hence to grow, depends on its savings rate. Savings provide the resources for investment. Figure 3–1 presents two rather discouraging comparisons for the United States. First, U.S. personal savings rates have averaged only about 6 percent of disposable income during the last 15 years, while households in the major OECD competitors studied here have been saving far more. Japanese savings have been about 20 percent of disposable incomes, German about 12 percent; even the British save more than Americans. The Canadian savings rate used to be as low as but is now far higher than the U.S. rate. In fact, the U.S. personal savings rate is the lowest on the graph by a rather large margin.

The second unfortunate comparison relates to trends. All of the other countries have shown clear upward trends in their savings rates, but there is almost no long-term trend in the U.S. rate which has fallen sharply since the mid-1970s. In 1979, Americans saved less than 5 percent of their incomes, which is hardly encouraging for future U.S. economic growth.

Retained earnings (business savings) have increased somewhat in recent years as U.S. businesses have not increased dividends to match increases in corporate profits. Although retained earnings have risen by over 10 percent as a share of U.S. corporate profits since the early 1960s, this has added just over 1 percentage point to the total savings rate (savings/GNP) of the economy (see Table 3–1). It does not even come close to offsetting the fact that household savings rates are far higher in the major OECD competitors than they are in the United States. Adding a percentage point of two to the U.S. savings rate would not change the conclusion that it is significantly lower than those prevailing in other major industrial countries.

POSSIBLE REASONS FOR LOW U.S. SAVINGS RATES

Until fairly recently, most economists relied on a very simple theory of household savings. Savings were a stable function of household income, and the proportion of income saved tended to rise slowly as real income rose. This historic Keynesian savings function has come under increasing attack from a number of sources. Friedman's permanent-income hypothesis suggested that consumption was a fairly stable function of what people believed to be their permanent income.[1] This means that transitory or "windfall" income will be saved and that temporary income losses will not cause consumption reductions. Savings will be reduced instead. The

---

[1] Friedman would include interest rates as a factor affecting a consumption/savings decision, but perceived levels of permanent income would be viewed as a far more important variable. See Milton Friedman, *A Theory of the Consumption Function* (Princeton, N.J.: Princeton University Press, 1956).

FIGURE 3-1. HOUSEHOLD SAVINGS RATIOS

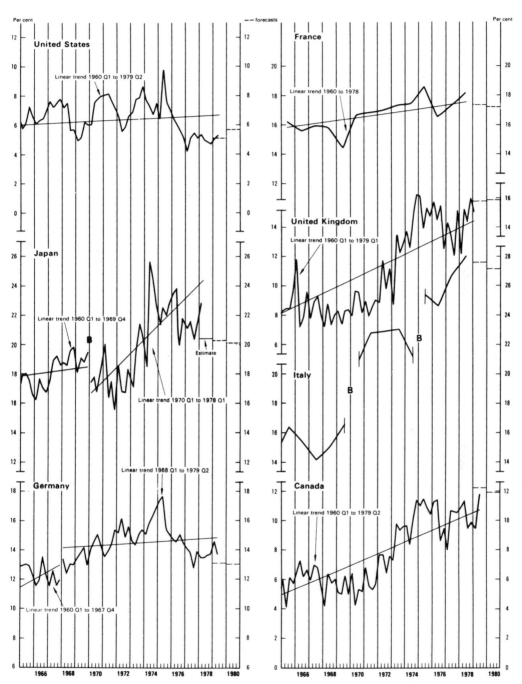

Source: OECD, *Economic Outlook* (December 1979), p. 134. Reproduced with permission.

permanent-income hypothesis suggests why temporary tax increases do not cut con-sumption; since people understand that the tax increase is temporary, they maintain consumption by cutting savings by the amount of the tax increase.

Recent theoretical literature suggests that savings decisions may be considerably more complex than either the Keynes or the Friedman models and that a number of factors other than current or permanent income are important in understanding savings rates.

Savings represent the decision to forgo current consumption in favor of future consumption for the saver or for the heirs. That decision may be undertaken for a number of reasons, one of which is the expectation that interest earned on the funds saved will allow somewhat more consumption in the future than would be possible at present. Except for minimum savings needed for old age and unforeseen emergencies, rational people cannot be expected to give up more consumption now for less consumption later. For the expectation of greater consumption opportunities in the future to encourage savings, real aftertax interest rates must be positive. A situation in which Americans are offered 6 percent on a passbook

TABLE 3-1. RETAINED CORPORATE EARNINGS IN THE UNITED STATES, 1960–79

	Retained Earnings ($ Billions)	Share of GNP (Percent)	Share of Aftertax Corporate Profits (Percent)
1960	$13.0	2.6%	50.4%
1961	12.5	2.4	48.4
1962	15.2	2.7	51.4
1963	16.0	2.7	50.8
1964	19.4	3.1	52.9
1965	25.2	3.7	56.9
1966	27.6	3.7	58.6
1967	24.7	3.1	55.0
1968	24.2	2.8	52.4
1969	21.2	2.3	48.4
1970	14.1	1.4	38.1
1971	21.3	2.0	48.1
1972	30.0	2.6	54.9
1973	39.3	3.0	58.6
1974	43.6	3.1	58.5
1975	38.7	2.5	54.8
1976	54.7	3.2	59.3
1977	62.4	3.3	59.7
1978	74.3	3.5	61.2
1979*	91.7	3.9	63.5

*Preliminary.
Source: *Economic Report of the President, 1980*, pp. 203 and 225.

TABLE 3-2. ESTIMATED REAL AFTERTAX U.S. INTEREST RATES: LONG-TERM FEDERAL BONDS, 1960-79*

1960	1.0%	1970	− 1.6%
1961	1.5	1971	− 0.6
1962	1.7	1972	0.4
1963	1.4	1973	− 1.7
1964	1.4	1974	− 5.9
1965	1.1	1975	− 4.2
1966	0.1	1976	− 1.4
1967	0.3	1977	− 1.8
1968	− 0.8	1978	− 3.5
1969	− 1.4	1979**	− 7.1

*These estimates assume a marginal personal tax rate of 35 percent, so the estimated real yield is 0.65 x nominal yield minus the percentage change in the consumer price index. These should be viewed as *ex post* real interest rates. Individuals will expect different real yields at the time they purchase bonds if they expect the rate of inflation to change.
**Estimated on the basis of data through August 1979.
Source: IMF, *International Financial Statistics*, line 61.

account or savings bond, which is fully taxable, while inflation is reducing the purchasing power of their capital at the rate of 9 or 10 percent a year is unlikely to encourage people to save. Table 3–2 indicates what people have earned (ex post) on long-term government bonds in recent years under the assumption that owners of bonds faced marginal tax rates of 35 percent. The assumed tax rate is probably low for the average holder of bonds, so the estimated real aftertax interest rates are probably a little high.

American savers have taken an awesome beating in recent years. The combination of rapid inflation and the fact that income taxes on interest income are not indexed for inflation has produced negative yields, which obviously encourages people to consume more and save less if they expect such negative yields to continue. When inflation rates were low, the typical U.S. saver probably viewed interest rates in nominal terms, that is, without mentally deducting the rate of inflation. In recent years, however, Americans have probably started to view interest payments as would citizens of Argentina or Brazil, that is, in real rather than nominal terms. U.S. inflation has become so much more rapid that U.S. residents have quickly lost their "money illusion" and have started automatically to adjust interest rates and other sources of income for inflation. People are now fully aware that U.S. aftertax real interest rates are negative, and the current U.S. savings rate reflects that understanding. It is not a coincidence that the U.S. personal savings rate fell sharply in the mid-1970s when U.S. inflation accelerated and real yields on most financial assets became negative.

Americans who have saved in order to invest in common stocks have done no better than those who have bought bonds. Dividend yields have typically been lower than bond yields, and common stock averages, such as the Dow Jones industrials, show declines since the late 1960s. Common stock prices have declined during a decade in which the price level has almost doubled. The effect on the real wealth of those holding equities, or those dependent on pension funds that have been invested in equities, has been striking and negative.

Recent press reports suggest that U.S. inflation is now encouraging a widespread use of new savings to purchase gold coins, art works and a variety of collectibles rather than financial assets. This represents a form of savings and investment which is totally unproductive. It has been common in many developing countries such as India, where personal wealth is widely held in the form of gold. Savings which are held in the form of such commodities or "collectibles" adds nothing to the ability of the economy to invest in productive plant and equipment. The savings/investment equality is maintained in this case via investment in increased inventories of commodities which produce nothing. It is discouraging to see U.S. inflation become such a detriment to the holding of financial assets that Americans are encouraged to make unproductive investments in increased commodity hoards. It is bad enough for the savings rate to be low; it is worse when whatever saving does occur ends up in the form of newly minted gold coins or "limited edition" porcelain figures.

SOCIAL SECURITY AND THE SAVINGS RATE

The financial needs of old age and the possibility of unforeseen medical or other emergency costs obviously constitute a major reason for saving.[2] People save during their working years (particularly during their late working years when family costs are low) and dissave after retirement. Some of this saving is institutionalized through contributory pension plans, and the remainder is informal. To the extent that government provides guaranteed retirement income through social security and protection against unforeseen medical costs through medicare or medicaid, the incentive to save for old age or for medical emergencies is obviously reduced. The establishment of universal national health insurance would remove one more reason for saving.

Saving is often intended to protect against a "rainy day." The rapid expansion of the social security system and massive increase in transfer payments resulting from the "Great Society" are intended to guarantee that Americans will not face any financially demanding rainy days. Research by Martin Feldstein indicates quite clearly that expansion of such programs does discourage personal savings—which should hardly be surprising.[3] In 1960, transfer payments totaled $29 billion, or just over 8 percent of all U.S. personal disposable incomes. In 1977, the total was $207 billion, or about 16 percent of all such incomes. Social security is by far the largest of the transfer payment programs. The rapid improvement of social security benefits and the growth of other transfer payment programs have undoubtedly

---

2   See Michael Boskin, "Social Security and Retirement Decisions" (Economic Inquiry, 1977) for an analysis of the effect of the social security system on savings. A more recent study by L.S. Kotlihoff, "Testing the Theory of Social Security and Life Cycle Accumulations" (American Economic Review, June 1979) also deals with this subject.

3   For example, see Martin Feldstein, "Social Security Induced Retirement and Aggregate Capital Accumulation," Journal of Political Economy (September/October 1974).

produced major short-term welfare gains in the United States. They have, however, had a major cost which was not foreseen when they were enacted. They have discouraged personal savings, lowered investment and thereby reduced output and income.

A social security system does not have to discourage savings; if run properly, it would *increase* savings. Such a social security system would be run like a private pension system, in which each pension would come from funds that the individuals and the employer had contributed during the employee's working lifetime. Under this arrangement, the social security system would produce a vast amount of savings as workers contributed to a fund for their own later retirement. If, as is currently the situation, each worker's contribution is instead used to finance the pensions of others who are currently retired, the system does not build up assets and no savings occur. This year's contributions by current workers are used to pay for this year's pensions for the currently retired, and a pure transfer payment rather than a form of forced saving results.

In recent decades, the U.S. social security system has operated entirely on the transfer payment rather than a forced-savings approach, and it has actually produced negative saving. Funds which were built up in an earlier period when contributions exceeded pension payments have been partially used up, and the system is now using current receipts to make current payments.[4] Workers may think that they are saving for their old age when they pay social security taxes, but they are in fact doing no such thing. They are instead providing transfer payments to those who are now retired with the expectation (or hope) that another generation of workers will be willing and able to provide transfer payments for them later in their lives. No saving is occurring.

The age structure of the U.S. adult population now represents a temporary factor in reducing savings rates. Young adults typically save very little and often dissave in order to purchase consumer durables when they set up new households. Savings occur later as the purchase of their consumer durables is completed and as incomes rise. Savings further increase when the raising and education of children is completed, before falling at retirement.[5] The U.S. population now includes an unusually large number of young adults and, consequently, it is experiencing a very rapid rate of household formation. Those forming new households do not save much and instead often dissave. As the baby-boom age cohorts grow older, they will probably save much more. Then, smaller age cohorts will be young adults who will save very little. Thus, U.S. savings rates can be expected to increase automatically in the late 1980s as the average age of the U.S. adult population rises.

Savings patterns are in part a reflection of national or group values. Economic theory says little in this area, but history suggests that if the population of a nation is oriented toward the present, it will not think about or plan for the future. This

---

4   For data on the status of the Old Age, Survivors, and Disability Trust Funds see the *Statistical Abstract of the United States, 1966,* p. 293, *1970,* p. 289, and *1979,* p. 259. For the most recent data, see *Special Analysis Budget of the United States Government 1981,* p. 89. These trust funds reached a peak of $48.2 billion in 1975 and declined to $33.4 by 1979. They are expected to decline to $25.1 billion by late 1981.

5   A. Ando and F. Modigliani, "The Life Cycle Hypothesis of Savings: Aggregate Implications and Tests," *American Economic Review* (March 1963).

means that it will not save. Societies and groups that have a strong orientation toward the future, which means a willingness to sacrifice now to gain later, are obviously likely to have high savings rates. The United States used to view itself as such a future-oriented society, but it is not clear that this is as true today. The values of the late 1960s and the early 1970s, particularly among the young, are certainly much more short-term in nature. The "now generation" values of the 1970s probably have contributed to low savings rates. However, negative aftertax real interest rates and government programs to eliminate the possibility of rainy days for which people might save are undoubtedly far more important in explaining low U.S. savings rates. Indeed, taxes and transfer programs may themselves have helped to produce the change in national and group values noted above.

GOVERNMENT DEFICITS AS A FORM OF NEGATIVE SAVING

It was suggested earlier that private saving can be offset by public dissaving (budget deficits), resulting in levels of private investment below current private savings. U.S. federal deficits have been huge in recent years, and do not seem to follow the countercyclical pattern of the 1950s and early 1960s. In the past, the federal government ran deficits in periods of recession, but these deficits quickly declined or became small surpluses during cyclical recoveries. This pattern changed after 1965. In recent years, the federal government has run deficits at all stages of the business cycle, and the deficits have often been large. The U.S. Treasury borrowed slightly over $40 billion in new funds during fiscal 1978. Almost $30 billion of that was for the budget deficit and the other $10 billion was for "off-budget" items, such as the Export-Import Bank, FHMA and so forth (see Table 3-3).

In recent years, large federal deficits have in part been offset by state and local surpluses. Thus, the net borrowing requirements of the U.S. public sector as a whole were smaller than for the federal government. The state and local surplus have been partially concentrated in California, and Proposition 13 may eliminate that part of the surplus fairly quickly.

Table 3-4 attempts to present a consistent comparison of the public sectors of five major OECD countries, in which deficits and surpluses are measured as a percentage of GNP for each of the countries.

It is interesting to note from Table 3-3 that the U.S. public sector ran deficits in every year but two between 1965 and 1978, i.e., at all stages of the business cycle, while Table 3-4 indicates that most of the other countries ran surpluses somewhat more frequently. In the latter half of the 1970s, however, large deficits became almost universal except for the United States which was almost in balance in 1978; and for which preliminary data indicate a small surplus in 1979.

Table 3-4 would seem to suggest that the U.S. public sector has been less of an inhibiting factor than the public sectors of other major OECD countries during the latter half of the 1970s. This conclusion ignores the fact, however, that the public sectors of countries other than the United States include sizable productive enterprises, such as public utilities, and that a large portion of the government expenditure financed in part by borrowing were for productive plant and equipment investment in these sectors. The U.S. public sector, in contrast, does not own and manage many large productive enterprises and, as a result, a much higher percen-

TABLE 3-3. GOVERNMENT RECEIPTS AND EXPENDITURES, NATIONAL INCOME AND PRODUCT ACCOUNTS, 1929-79

(Billions of U.S. Dollars)

Calendar Year or Quarter	Total Government			Federal Government			State and Local Government		
	Receipts	Expenditures	Surplus or Deficit (−) National Income and Product Accounts	Receipts	Expenditures	Surplus or Deficit (−) National Income and Product Accounts	Receipts	Expenditures	Surplus or Deficit (−) National Income and Product Accounts
1929	$11.3	$10.3	$1.0	$3.8	$2.6	$1.2	$7.6	$7.8	− $0.2
1933	9.3	10.7	− 1.4	2.7	4.0	− 1.3	7.2	7.2	− .1
1939	15.4	17.6	− 2.2	6.7	8.9	− 2.2	9.6	9.6	0.0
1940	17.7	18.4	− 0.7	8.6	10.0	− 1.3	10.0	9.3	0.6
1942	32.6	64.0	− 31.4	22.9	56.1	− 33.1	10.6	8.8	1.8
1944	51.2	103.0	− 51.8	41.0	95.5	− 54.5	11.1	8.5	2.7
1946	51.0	45.6	5.4	39.1	35.6	3.5	13.0	11.1	1.9
1948	58.9	50.5	8.4	43.2	34.9	8.3	17.7	17.6	1.0
1950	69.0	61.0	8.0	50.0	40.8	9.2	21.3	22.5	− 1.2
1951	85.2	79.2	6.1	64.3	57.8	6.5	23.4	23.9	− 0.4
1952	90.1	93.9	− 3.8	67.3	71.1	− 3.7	25.4	25.5	− 0.0
1953	94.6	101.6	− 6.9	70.0	77.1	− 7.1	27.4	27.3	0.1
1954	89.9	97.0	− 7.1	63.7	69.8	− 6.0	29.0	30.2	− 1.1
1955	101.1	98.0	3.1	72.6	68.1	4.4	31.7	32.9	− 1.3
1956	109.7	104.5	5.2	78.0	71.9	6.1	35.0	35.9	− 0.9
1957	116.2	115.3	.9	81.9	79.6	2.3	38.5	39.8	− 1.4
1958	115.0	127.6	− 12.6	78.7	88.9	− 10.3	42.0	44.3	− 2.4
1959	129.4	131.0	− 1.6	89.8	91.0	− 1.1	46.4	46.9	− 0.4
1960	139.5	136.4	3.1	96.1	93.1	3.0	49.9	49.8	0.1
1961	144.8	149.1	− 4.3	98.1	101.9	− 3.9	54.0	54.4	− 0.4
1962	156.7	160.5	− 3.8	106.2	110.4	− 4.2	58.5	58.0	0.5
1963	168.5	167.8	.7	114.4	114.2	0.3	63.2	62.8	0.5
1964	174.0	176.3	− 2.3	114.9	118.2	− 3.3	69.5	68.5	1.0
1965	183.3	187.8	0.5	124.3	123.8	0.5	75.1	75.1	− 0.0
1966	212.3	213.6	− 1.3	141.8	143.6	− 1.8	84.8	84.3	0.5
1967	228.2	242.4	− 14.2	150.5	163.7	− 13.2	93.6	94.7	− 1.1
1968	263.4	268.9	− 5.5	174.7	180.6	− 5.8	107.2	106.9	0.3
1969	296.3	285.6	10.7	197.0	188.4	8.5	119.7	117.6	2.1
1970	302.6	311.9	− 9.4	192.1	204.2	− 12.1	134.9	132.2	2.8
1971	322.2	340.5	− 18.3	198.6	220.6	− 22.0	152.6	148.9	3.7
1972	367.4	370.9	− 3.5	227.5	244.7	− 17.3	177.4	163.7	13.7
1973	411.2	404.9	6.3	258.3	265.0	− 6.7	193.5	180.5	13.0
1974	455.1	458.2	− 3.2	288.6	299.3	− 10.7	210.4	202.8	7.6
1975	468.5	532.8	− 64.4	286.2	356.8	− 70.6	236.9	230.6	6.2
1976	538.3	574.0	− 35.7	331.4	385.0	− 53.6	268.0	250.1	17.9
1977	606.6	626.1	− 19.5	375.4	421.7	− 46.3	298.8	271.9	26.8
1978	685.7	686.0	− 0.3	432.1	459.8	− 27.7	331.0	303.6	27.4
1979*	771.9	757.9	14.0	497.6	503.0	− 10.5	354.4	329.9	24.4

Note: Federal grants-in-aid to state and local governments are reflected in federal expenditures and state and local receipts. Total government receipts and expenditures have been adjusted to eliminate this duplication.
*Preliminary.
Source: *Economic Report of the President, 1980*, p. 288.

TABLE 3-4.   PUBLIC-SECTOR SURPLUS OR DEFICIT (−) AS A PERCENTAGE OF GNP*

	1963–69	1970–73	1974	1975	1976	1977	1978	1979**
U.S.	0.0%	− 0.2%	− 0.3%	−4.5%	−2.1%	− 1.0%	0.0%	+ 0.4%
Canada	+ 0.8	+ 0.6	+ 0.4	− 2.9	− 1.8	− 2.9	− 3.9	− 3.1
France	+ 0.4	+ 0.8	+ 0.6	− 2.2	− 0.5	− 1.3	− 2.3	− 1.9
Italy	− 2.8	− 5.4	− 5.4	− 11.1	− 9.1	− 8.1	− 10.6	− 11.1
Japan	− 2.7	+ 0.9	+ 0.2	− 4.3	− 3.6	− 3.9	− 5.0	− 4.9
U.K.	− 0.9	− 0.7	− 5.3	− 5.7	− 5.0	− 3.2	− 4.2	− 3.4
West Germany	− 0.2	+ 0.3	− 1.2	− 6.3	− 3.6	− 2.6	− 2.8	− 3.1

*The 1964–73 data appear to be based on slightly different definitions and are not directly comparable with the 1974–80 data. The 1964–73 definitions appear to produce smaller deficits, and the 1974–79 data for the United States are close to those found in Table 3-3 which is drawn from the 1980 *Economic Report of the President.*
**OECD forecasts.
Sources: 1964–73, OECD, *Economic Outlook* (September 1979), p. 143; 1974–75, OECD, *Economic Outlook* (July 1976), p. 25; and 1976–80, OECD, *Economic Outlook* (December 1979), p. 34.

tage of U.S. government expenditures are pure public consumption. The public sectors of the other OECD countries may be borrowing a higher percentage of GNP than the United States, but a significant part of their borrowing is to finance productive investment in government-owned utilities and other enterprises.

The U.S. government both borrows to finance its own deficits and has major effects on the allocation of the funds which remain available to the private sector through a variety of regulatory techniques. Loan guarantees have been provided for some sectors of the economy such as housing and student loans as well as to Chrysler, and in other areas the government encourages private financial institutions to favor particular groups of borrowers. Politicians and interest groups typically view loan guarantees as a free good because they do not impose budgetary costs on the government if the loans are repaid, but funds which are diverted to favored sectors are necessarily unavailable for other potentially more productive investments. According to a recent press report, the federal government has guaranteed or otherwise subsidized almost 10 percent of all private borrowing in the U.S. economy.[6] If the allocation of funds among private borrowers is not regulated, guaranteed or otherwise distorted, funds flow to those uses which provide the highest prospective rate of return after allowance for risk. Whenever Washington decides to guarantee one sector's (or one company's) borrowing, some of these higher rate-of-return projects are shut out of the capital market, and the economy grows more slowly. Loan guarantees are not free; their cost is the more productive uses of funds and resources which become impossible because of the needs of the favored sectors of the economy.

6   Bradley Graham, "Federal Loan Guarantees Arouse Economic Concern," *The Washington Post* (August 20, 1979), p. 1.

THE CURRENT ACCOUNT AS A SOURCE OF FINANCING FOR INVESTMENT

It was suggested earlier that an economy is not limited to investing only what it saves if it can maintain and finance a current-account deficit. That deficit becomes a source of real resources which make possible levels of investment in excess of domestic savings.

Table 3–5 shows that, during the 1960s, the group of OECD countries studied here ran average current-account surpluses of about $4.5 billion. This means that they invested domestically that much less than they saved. The United States dominated the list with an average annual surplus of $3.3 billion. France and Canada were net borrowers from the rest of the world, while Germany, Italy and Japan were net lenders. In the 1970s, this pattern changed radically. The United States ran a combined current-account surplus from 1970 to 1976 which totaled about $30 billion, whereas it ran a slightly larger deficit from 1977 through 1979. During these three years, the United States borrowed over $30 billion from the rest of the world in order to finance an excess of investment over domestic savings of that amount. Canada ran a total current-account deficit of about $24 billion during the 1970–79 period. The size of Canadian net borrowing from the rest of the world becomes striking when it is noted that the Canadian economy is about one-tenth the

TABLE 3-5. CURRENT-ACCOUNT BALANCES, 1960-79[a]
(Millions of U.S. Dollars)

	1960	1961	1962	1963	1964	1965	1966	1967	1968	1969
U.S.	$2,824	$3,821	$3,383	$4,414	$6,822	$5,431	$3,029	$2,584	$611	$399
Canada	− 1,272	− 916	− 776	− 483	− 394	− 1,050	− 1,079	-463	− 91	− 850
France	146	187	− 84	− 344	− 760	353	− 255	205	− 855	− 1,475
Italy	283	474	236	− 746	620	2,209	2,117	1,599	2,627	2,340
Japan	140	− 982	− 48	-780	− 480	932	1,254	− 190	1,048	2,119
U.K.	− 685	61	358	367	− 996	− 72	291	− 805	− 687	1,112
West Germany	1,139	798	− 395	248	131	− 1,556	122	2,502	2,964	1,913
Total	2,575	3,443	2,679	2,676	4,943	6,247	5,479	5,432	5,617	5,558

	1970	1971	1972	1973	1974	1975	1976	1977	1978	1979[c]
U.S.	$2,340	− $1,419	− $5,744	$7,141	$4,851[b]	$18,339	$4,605	− $14,092	- $13,900	− $2,500
Canada	1,059	427	− 389	108	− 1,493	− 4,677	− 3,897	− 4,043	− 4,600	− 6,000
France	68	525	284	− 675	− 5,980	− 66	− 6,097	− 3,328	3,900	1,500
Italy	1,133	1,902	2,043	− 2,662	− 8,017	− 751	− 2,816	2,465	6,400	6,250
Japan	1,970	5,797	6,624	− 136	− 4,693	− 682	3,680	10,918	16,500	− 7,500
U.K.	1,754	2,653	338	− 2,592	− 8,575	− 4,106	− 1,511	511	2,000	− 5,500
West Germany	870	830	795	4,604	9,852	3,463	3,433	4,234	8,800	− 1,000
Total	9,194	10,715	3,681	5,788	-14,055	11,820	-2,603	-3,335	19,100	-14,750

[a]Goods, services and all transfer payments.

[b]Excluding cancellation of Indian debt (− 1993) and extraordinary grants (− 746).

[c]OECD forecasts.

Source: OECD, *Economic Outlook* (December 1979), p. 132 (1960–76) and p. 62 (1978–79).

size of the U.S. economy. The French and the British ran deficits in this period, but the amount of net borrowing was considerably smaller than the Canadian. Italy's deficit was approximately $6 billion.

Japan and Germany were massive lenders to the rest of the world in the 1970–79 period. Together, they ran a current-account surplus of over $68 billion during these years, which means that their economies saved that much more than they invested domestically. This pattern of investing considerably less than their economies save may be a significant cause of the declines in the rates of growth of labor productivity and real GNP in both economies during the 1970s. If the real capital stock of these economies had been $68 billion higher because all domestic savings had been invested domestically during this period, capital/labor ratios, labor productivity and real GNP would undoubtedly have been considerably higher. $68 billion is a great deal of real capital for only two countries to transfer to the rest of the world via current-account surpluses. In contrast, the United States neither exported nor imported a significant amount of capital during the decade of the 1970s.

The seven countries as a group ran a current-account surplus of about $25 billion during the 1970–79 period. The OPEC countries ran a huge surplus, the nonoil less-developed countries ran large deficits, and the major OECD countries were in modest surplus. The accumulated surplus of $25 billion for the group is small enough to suggest that outflows of resources through current-account surpluses were not a major impediment for investment and growth for these countries as a group.

Investment as a Source of Economic Growth

4

It was suggested earlier that there is likely to be a close relationship between the percentage of GNP a country invests and that country's rates of growth of labor productivity and of GNP per capita. The percentage of GNP which a country invests in new plant and equipment is probably the single most important determinant of its growth rate. Table 4-1 presents these investment ratios for the seven industrialized countries studied.

These numbers present a rather striking but not very pleasant conclusion for the United States. In the period from 1960 to 1978, the U.S. investment performance was last in 15 out of 19 years. In one year it was tied for last place, and in the other three it was next to last. The United Kingdom is widely viewed as a country with low savings and investment performance, but the U.K. investment ratio was an annual average of 18.0 percent, compared to 17.2 percent for the United States, during the 19-year period. A more striking contrast, of course, can be found between Japan and the United States. The Japanese invested an average of 32.2 percent of GNP during the 1960–78 period. This extraordinary performance occurred despite the fact that Japan ran an accumulated current-account surplus of $41.5 billion during this time.

TABLE 4-1. TOTAL INVESTMENT AS A PERCENTAGE OF GNP, 1960-78

	1960	1961	1962	1963	1964	1965	1966	1967	1968	1969
U.S.	17.6%	16.6%	18.4%	16.6%	16.7%	17.1%	17.0%	16.5%	16.6%	16.9%
Canada	22.9	20.4	22.0	20.9	22.4	24.1	25.1	23.9	21.7	21.6
France	20.4	19.7	20.4	22.2	23.8	24.4	25.0	25.1	24.8	25.4
Italy	23.2	23.9	24.1	23.5	21.7	18.8	18.3	18.9	19.7	20.5
Japan	27.5	34.4	27.1	32.2	32.6	30.7	31.0	32.2	33.5	34.7
U.K.	17.4	17.1	15.7	16.0	17.6	17.6	17.6	18.1	18.6	18.1
West Germany	26.0	25.9	25.0	25.2	26.4	26.3	25.4	22.8	23.1	24.2

	1970	1971	1972	1973	1974	1975	1976	1977	1978
U.S.	17.3%	17.7%	18.3%	18.4%	17.7%	16.2%	16.4%	17.4%	17.6%*
Canada	21.0	21.8	21.6	22.2	23.2	24.3	23.4	23.0	22.6
France	25.5	25.6	25.7	25.5	26.2	23.4	23.2	22.5	21.4
Italy	21.2	20.2	19.7	20.8	23.0	21.2	20.1	19.8	18.8
Japan	35.0	34.3	34.5	36.6	34.2	30.8	30.0	30.0	30.5
U.K.	18.3	18.3	18.3	19.3	20.0	19.7	18.9	17.9	18.1
West Germany	26.4	26.7	26.1	24.6	22.5	21.2	20.4	20.9	21.6

*Estimated using 1977 public investment and 1978 private investment as a percentage of 1978 GNP.
Source: IMF, *International Financial Statistics.* Line 93e divided by line 99a for all countries except the United States, where line 93gf plus 93ee divided by 99a is used. Private and public investment are listed separately for the United States, but not for the other countries.

The Japanese saved $41.5 billion more than they invested domestically and still managed an average investment ratio of 32.2 percent.

It is also interesting to note that the French investment ratios have often been very close to, and sometimes slightly above, those prevailing in Germany. France invested an average of 23.7 percent of GNP and Germany 24.3 percent during the 19 years. Italy and Canada were somewhat lower, but still well above the levels prevailing in the United States and the United Kingdom.

The other major conclusion of this table is that there was a slight convergence in the national investment ratios during the 1970s. The 1960s pattern in which the United States was last, Japan first and the others in the middle still holds, but the differences are slightly narrower. This change has occurred because the U.S. investment ratio has been fairly stable through the 1960s and '70s at 16 to 18 percent while the ratios have declined significantly in Japan and Germany. In the late 1960s and early 1970s, Japan was investing about 35 percent of GNP; for the last three years, this figure was 30 percent, a significant reduction. Germany was investing 26 percent of GNP a few years ago, and the figure is now 21 percent. In the late 1960s and early 1970s, the other countries were typically investing much more than the United States. Although they still have higher investment ratios than the United States, the differences are now less striking. The United States is, however, still last among the countries studied—with all that this implies for capital/labor ratios, for the age of the capital stock and for the technology that is embodied in it.

LOW U.S. INVESTMENT RATIOS: POSSIBLE CAUSES

Any explanation of low levels of U.S. investment in plant and equipment should begin with the low levels of savings discussed earlier. If the U.S. economy consumes (privately and publicly) the vast majority of what it produces, there simply are not enough real resources left over for adequate levels of productive investment when the economy is close to full employment. Supply constraints become a very real limitation on investment.

This problem is particularly apparent during strong cyclical recoveries, such as 1976–78. Business intentions to invest usually rise during these recoveries, as they did in the latter phase of the 1976–78 recovery, but consumer demand was so strong that shortages of raw materials and other goods developed that made it hard to complete investment projects. Although savings rates normally are expected to be fairly high in a recovery (thus making resources available for investment), U.S. consumer demand was so strong in this period that the economy simply consumed almost all of what it produced, leaving insufficient resources for normal cyclical increases in investment. Backlogs grew, delivery dates stretched out, and the economy hit full capacity in many sectors without a real investment boom. Because other major OECD countries save far more than the United States, much higher levels of investment are possible late in cyclical recoveries without supply constraints.

The other side of the investment question deals with factors that may discourage U.S. businesses from undertaking major plant and equipment investments. Although such investment decisions are complex and far from being perfectly understood, analysis begins with the proposition that firms invest when they expect the profit rate on a project to exceed the cost of borrowing or otherwise raising the necessary funds and when the project is not excessively risky, that is, when the firm is fairly certain that its expected yield will be realized. The greater the riskiness of the project, the greater the margin must be between the expected profit rate and the cost of funds to encourage a positive decision.

Precise comparisons of rates of profit among countries are very difficult due to differences in accounting systems and the lack of regularly published data. Although net rates of return on invested capital or equity are not available for the countries in this study, gross profits as a percentage of corporate value added represent a reasonable substitute, and time series for this measure of profits were developed for a recent OECD study.

Table 4–2 does not suggest that there has been a clear trend in the profit share for the United States. 1960 and 1975 were both recession years, and the figures for these two years are fairly similar. Profit levels were obviously quite high in the mid-1960s and have not been as strong since then. Canada, France and Germany also lack any apparent trend in profit shares, although returns to capital have typically been a higher percentage of corporate value added in all three of these countries than in the United States. There is a modest downward trend in the figures for Japan, but profit rates have remained considerably higher there compared to the other countries studied. A somewhat sharper decline is apparent in Italy, and an even more extreme reduction in profit shares is apparent in the United Kingdom.

Comparing profit rates across countries, U.S. profit rates have recently been lower than those in all of the other countries except Italy and the United Kingdom.

TABLE 4-2. GROSS PROFIT SHARE, 1960–76
(Percent)

Year	U.S.	Canada	France	Italy	Japan	U.K.	W. Ger.
1960	25.7%	26.4%	31.5%	33.5%	42.7%	23.8%	28.0%
1961	26.1	26.4	30.6	34.7	43.9	21.8	27.6
1962	27.6	27.1	29.3	32.7	41.4	21.7	27.1
1963	28.1	27.7	29.1	30.0	41.6	23.3	27.2
1964	28.5	28.7	29.5	29.7	41.4	23.2	27.4
1965	29.5	28.2	29.2	31.6	39.7	22.3	27.2
1966	29.2	27.3	30.2	32.7	41.1	20.4	27.2
1967	28.2	26.3	30.3	31.8	42.1	20.9	27.8
1968	27.6	27.0	31.3	32.4	43.6	20.7	28.9
1969	26.0	26.5	32.3	32.2	43.7	19.2	28.6
1970	24.3	24.7	32.6	29.4	43.7	17.1	27.6
1971	25.3	24.8	32.5	26.4	41.8	17.9	26.9
1972	26.2	26.0	32.5	26.1	40.5	17.8	26.6
1973	25.0	28.8	31.9	25.4	36.8	16.8	26.1
1974	23.6	30.2	32.8	23.0	36.6	12.3	25.6
1975	24.6	27.8	32.3	22.3	37.6	11.4	26.0
1976*	25.1	27.2	32.7	22.2	40.8	11.4	28.0

*1976 figures are estimates.

Note: *Gross profit share* is defined as the gross property income share in the corporate value added. Years are calendar years except for Japan for which fiscal years run from April 1 to March 31 of the next calendar year.

Source: OECD, *Towards Full Employment and Price Stability* (July 1977), p. 307. Reprinted with permission.

Canadian and German profit rates, however, have been only slightly higher than those in the United States. Japanese and French profits have been considerably higher than those prevailing elsewhere.

The figures in Table 4–2 are for gross profits as a share of corporate value added, which raises a question with regard to rates of return on equity. If capital/output ratios have been rising in the major OECD countries, due to investment levels that have been sufficient to increase the size of the capital stock faster than output has grown, then the lack of any upward trend in profits as a percentage of output would imply a decline in rates of return on capital. This is particularly likely in Japan, Germany and France, where investment has been a high percentage of GNP and where the capital stock has consequently grown very rapidly. In the United States, however, where investment has been a considerably lower percentage of GNP, the capital/output ratio has not grown as rapidly (it may not have grown at all during the last few years), so the lack of a clear trend in profits as a share of output would not suggest a significant decline in rates of return on equity.

Table 4–3 presents data on U.S. aftertax profits as a percentage of net worth for the manufacturing sector of the economy. There is no apparent trend in the U.S. rates of return on net worth. The cyclical component in the series is evident in that every recent recession can be seen as a decline in profit rates, but it does not appear that there has been any long-term trend in profit rates.[1] This parallels the conclusion of a recent study by Scott Brown who suggested that cyclically adjusted profit shares did not show a secular trend in the United States in the 1950–75 period.[2]

Although profit rates do not appear to have declined in the United States, the cost of raising money to finance plant and equipment has increased sharply and has become a major problem.[3] Interest rates on long-term corporate bonds have increased from 3 percent in the early 1950s to well above 10 percent in 1980. It has become extremely expensive to borrow long-term funds for plant and equipment investments, and profit rates do not appear to have increased to offset this additional cost (see Table 4–4).[4]

---

1   Data on U.S. profit rates come from more than one source, and the published figures sometimes seem contradictory. The data in Table 4–3, which suggest no decline in U.S. rates of return on equity in the manufacturing sector, is from the Federal Trade Commission. The Department of Commerce and the Department of Labor provide data on returns to capital as a share of corporate output (Table B–12 on page 217 of the 1980 Economic Report of the President) which indicate a decline in the share of such output going to capital. The difference between the apparent conclusions of the two tables may be the result of declining capital to output ratios in the corporate sector, or declines in profit rates in the nonmanufacturing corporate sector relative to manufacturing. It may also be the result of increasing debt to equity ratios which make it possible for rates of return on equity to remain stable despite a decline in the total return to capital. To the extent to which U.S. corporations still have bonds outstanding which bear the low interest rates prevailing in the early and mid-1960s, rates of return on equity would be increased relative to the return on all capital. One can only conclude that trends in profits depend in part on which data one uses, but that rates of return on equity in manufacturing have not shown a clear trend.

2   Scott Brown, "Cyclical Fluctuations in the Share of Corporate Profits in National Income," Kyklos (Fasc. 2), 1978.

3   For a discussion of how the productivity of capital and the cost of capital influence investment, see Robert Lucas, Jr. and E.C. Prescott, "Investment Under Uncertainty," Econometrica (1971).

4   It might be argued that recent rates of inflation made the real cost of borrowing extremely low. A 9 percent interest rate in a period of 12 percent inflation would appear very attractive, and might lead to the conclusion that firms should

(Continued)

TABLE 4-3. AFTERTAX PROFITS AS A PERCENTAGE OF NET WORTH IN U.S. MANUFACTURING, 1950-79

Year	%	Year	%
1950	15.4%	1965	13.0%
1951	12.1	1966	13.4
1952	10.3	1967	11.7
1953	10.5	1968	12.1
1954	9.9	1969	11.5
1955	12.6	1970	9.3
1956	12.3	1971	9.7
1957	10.9	1972	10.6
1958	8.6	1973	12.8
1959	10.4	1974*	14.9
1960	9.2	1975	11.6
1961	8.9	1976	13.9
1962	9.8	1977	14.2
1963	10.3	1978	15.0
1964	11.6	1979 (I-III)	16.7

*New series. It appears that the data in the new series (1974-79) is about 1 percent higher than that provided for previous years. Subtracting 1 percent from the 1974-79 data would seem to make it more comparable to the earlier period.

Source: *Economic Report of the President, 1980*, p. 301.

The cost of raising equity funds has recently become at least as much of a problem as the cost of borrowing. During the mid- and late 1970s, the common stocks of many apparently sound companies sold for less than book value, which made it impossible to sell new shares without reducing net worth per share for previous investors, i.e., watering the stock. Table 4-5 shows that price/earnings ratios of 14 to 20 were common as recently as the early 1970s, but were not typical in the mid-1970s. The price/earnings ratio on the Dow Jones industrial averages was 6.8 in July 1979 compared to 9.6 a year earlier.[5] When a firm can only sell new shares at seven times earnings, it becomes terribly expensive to raise new equity funds. As a result, the new issues market has been very quiet, and few firms are

---

(Footnote 4 continued)
be eagerly borrowing for new plant and equipment investments. There are two problems with this argument: first, firms are interested in the margin between what productive assets earn and what it costs to finance them, and since there is little evidence that nominal rates of return on fixed assets have increased significantly, the margin between expected earnings and borrowing costs has been narrowed. Second, firms cannot assume that current rates of inflation will continue over the life of a bond issue, and this means that real interest rates may turn out to be far higher in the long run than in the short. Borrowing for 20 years at 9 or 10 percent may be attractive if the borrower can be certain that inflation will remain at its current rate for the next two decades. If rates of inflation return to earlier levels of 3 or 4 percent, however, the 9 or 10 percent nominal interest rate becomes 6 percent in real terms which is very expensive financing. Since firms have no way of knowing what will happen to inflation rates and hence to the rate at which the assets they finance with borrowed money will increase in value, they are likely to be discouraged from making major investments in plant and equipment by high nominal interest rates in periods of rapid current inflation.

5   *Wall Street Journal* (July 30, 1979), p. 31.

bringing secondary issues to market. The sale of new common stock has ceased to be a major source of financing for plant and equipment investment, which discourages such undertakings. Many firms have been borrowing heavily despite high interest rates, but this has produced debt/equity ratios which may be higher than would be prudent. Equity has been built up to a modest degree through increases in retained earnings but stockholders are understandably annoyed to see their dividends fail to keep up with inflation, particularly since the behavior of the stock market has meant that few of them are earning capital gains. Consequently, firms are under stockholder pressure for higher dividends, which limits their ability to use retained earnings as a way to reduce debt/equity ratios.

To summarize, U.S. profit rates by themselves, measured as returns on equity or sales, do not seem to have discouraged investment. There has been no downward trend in either series, and profit rates have held up quite well compared to other major OECD countries. The cost of raising capital, however, has been a problem. Corporate bond rates have risen sharply since the early 1960s, making it more expensive to borrow long-term funds for plant and equipment investments. In recent years, price/earnings ratios on U.S. common stocks have fallen sharply, making it almost impossibly expensive to sell new shares to finance growth. Selling equity at 7 times earnings, which implies an ultimate yield to the stockholder of over 14 percent, is worse than unattractive. It has also become very difficult to sell common stocks of new or unknown firms to the public, which strongly discourages the growth of young firms (Xerox or Polaroid of 25 years ago). This slows the growth of the economy now and in the future. Low price/earnings ratios have also discouraged additional sales of common stocks by large established firms, forcing them to rely on borrowed funds or retained earnings for growth. High debt/equity ratios are widely viewed as unsafe, and this has become a problem that has probably limited the growth of many companies.

TABLE 4-4. U.S. CORPORATE BOND YIELDS (Aaa), 1950-79

Year	Yield	Year	Yield
1950	2.6%	1965	4.5%
1951	2.9	1966	5.1
1952	3.0	1967	5.5
1953	3.2	1968	6.2
1954	2.9	1969	7.0
1955	3.1	1970	8.0
1956	3.4	1971	7.4
1957	3.9	1972	7.2
1958	3.8	1973	7.4
		1974	8.6
1960	4.4	1975	8.8
1961	4.4	1976	8.4
1962	4.3	1977	8.0
1963	4.3	1978	8.7
1964	4.4	1979	9.6

Source: *Economic Report of the President, 1980*, p. 78.

TABLE 4-5. U.S. COMMON STOCKS: PRICE/AVERAGE EARNINGS RATIOS, STANDARD AND POORS 500 STOCKS, 1950-78

1950	7.1	1965	17.9
1951	8.5	1966	15.1
1952	10.6	1967	17.4
1953	9.7	1968	17.6
1954	11.7	1969	16.4
1955	12.6	1970	15.5
1956	13.2	1971	18.5
1957	12.7	1972	18.2
1958	16.1	1973	14.0
1959	17.3	1974	8.6
1960	16.9	1975	10.9
1961	21.6	1976	11.2
1962	17.2	1977	9.3
1963	18.2	1978	8.3
1964	18.8		

Source: *Economic Report of the President, 1980*, p. 307.

The increased cost of funds for investment basically represents the scarcity of resources implied by low personal savings rates and by public dissaving at the federal level. If savings rates were higher and if the public sector borrowed less, the costs of raising funds via equity or debt would fall, and investment in plant and equipment would be strongly encouraged.

LABOR COSTS AND INVESTMENT

Capital and labor are substitutes in most productive processes, so a company's decision to make investments can often be positively related to the cost of labor. When wages are high and expected to increase further relative to the cost of capital, firms avoid hiring more workers by installing more automated and hence less labor-intensive equipment. Lower wages relative to the cost of capital will encourage firms to stay with old equipment and expand production by hiring more labor, often through an extra shift or overtime.

Table 4-6 indicates that real wage rates (cash wages adjusted for inflation) have increased sharply in most other OECD countries, which has provided a strong incentive for further investment in automated equipment to avoid hiring more workers. In the United States, in contrast, real wages actually fell between 1972 and 1976. Nominal wages obviously rose, but this increase was more than offset by inflation. Preliminary data suggest a very slight increase in U.S. real wage rates in 1977 and 1978 (less than 1 percent a year), so real wages remained slightly below 1972 levels at the end of 1978, and almost certainly fell during 1979.

The reasons for the difference between U.S. and other OECD wage behavior is not hard to understand. Table 4-7 shows that the U.S. labor force has increased very rapidly during recent years because of a combination of much higher participation rates of women and the arrival of the postwar baby boom at working age. Except for Canada, labor-force growth was far slower in the other OECD countries.

The rapid increase in the supply of labor in the United States had exactly the effect economic theory would suggest: real wage rates were held down and companies were encouraged to substitute labor for capital, that is, to avoid expensive automation in favor of hiring more workers to run existing equipment. In addition, there has been a rapid growth of small labor-intensive firms in the services sector of the U.S. economy. The number of Americans employed has risen very rapidly, the capital stock less rapidly, and both labor productivity and real wage rates were held down as a result. This is a natural and predictable response to a large increase in the U.S. labor force.[6] The period of rapid growth in the labor force is almost at an end, however, so this process will not continue for long. During the latter half of the 1980s, increased output is going to require more capital since large increases in the labor force will no longer be possible.

U.S. firms have also been encouraged to hire more labor instead of investing in permanent plant and equipment by the relative ease of reducing the number of people employed in periods of recession. The United States does not have laws or traditions limiting the ability of firms to lay people off when business declines, but the situation is quite different elsewhere. European labor unions and governments have made it increasingly difficult and expensive for a firm to reduce the number of people it employs. Prior notice must be given, large separation payments must be made to those losing jobs, and in some cases, it is almost impossible to shut down a plant. In Japan, a strong tradition of lifetime employment makes it difficult or impossible for firms to reduce quickly the number of people they employ. In

TABLE 4-6. INCREASES IN REAL WAGES, 1972-76

	Productivity[a]	National Income Norm[b]	Real Wages[c]
U.S.	2.4%	1.2%	− 2.0%
Canada	3.5	6.5	12.7
France	12.8	11.0	16.3
Italy	8.8	1.9	9.4
Japan	14.8	9.1	20.3
U.K.	5.5	1.7	10.2
West Germany	15.2	13.4	12.6

[a]GDP in real dollars per head of total employment.
[b]Productivity adjusted for real terms of trade effect.
[c]Nominal wages and salaries deflated by consumer price index per head of employment.
Source: OECD, *Economic Surveys* (1978), p. 24.

---

6   Data presented in the *Morgan Guaranty Survey* (September 1979, p. 12) indicate that the U.S. capital/labor ratio rose steadily from 1948 to the late 1960s, rose less rapidly in the early 1970s, and actually declined after 1976.

**TABLE 4-7. CIVILIAN LABOR FORCES, EMPLOYMENT
AND UNEMPLOYMENT**
(Average Annual Percent Changes,
1958–68 and 1969–78)

	Labor Force	Employment	Unemployment
United States			
1958–68	1.5%	1.9%	− 4.8%
1969–78	2.4	2.1	8.8
Canada			
1958–68	2.6	2.8	− 1.4
1969–78	3.2	2.8	10.1
France			
1958–68	0.6	0.5	8.8
1969–78	0.9	0.4	14.7
Italy			
1958–68	−1.0	− 0.7	− 6.4
1969–78	1.4	0.9	10.2
Japan			
1958–68	1.4	1.5	− 4.1
1969–78	0.9	0.8	9.0
United Kingdom			
1958–68	0.4	0.3	2.9
1969–78	0.4	0.1	12.0
West Germany			
1958–68	0.1	0.1	−8.4
1969–78	−0.1	−0.5	21.0

Source: OECD, *Labor Force Statistics* (annual), various issues.

addition, effective payroll taxes are much higher in Europe and Japan than in the United States. As a result of these restrictions and high payroll taxes, Japanese and European firms are strongly discouraged from hiring more people unless they are certain that they will be needed permanently. Since such certainty is usually impossible, firms are encouraged to avoid hiring additional workers and instead to use more capital as a substitute for labor. More mechanization and automation thus become preferable to hiring more workers, and high rates of plant and equipment investment are accompanied by stagnating levels of employment, the departure of "guest workers," and relatively high unemployment rates in many European countries.

ENVIRONMENTAL REGULATION AND RETURNS TO INVESTMENT

The rapid increase in the requirements that U.S. environmental protection laws and regulations place on businesses has had a depressing effect on U.S. investment by creating a major difference between private and social returns from plant and equipment expenditures. From the perspective of society at large, for example, investments in air and water pollution control equipment may be very productive, that is, they may have a real yield to society which more than justifies their costs. From the viewpoint of the firm making the investment, however, such pollution control equipment is not productive or profitable. The benefits accrue to society at large, but the costs are borne by the investor or by the customers through higher prices.[7] A great deal of recent U.S. investment has added nothing to firms' capacity to produce output that can be sold, but has added to society's welfare in the form of cleaner air and water. The important point is that GNP data do not reflect these welfare improvements, for reasons discussed earlier, and as a result, the costs of such regulations show up as additional inflation (if market conditions allow the firm fully to pass on the costs of regulation) or as reduced profitability for plant and equipment investments. Where an increase in imports or other market conditions do not allow a full pass-through of costs imposed by environmental regulations, profit rates fall and firms are clearly discouraged from investing in new plant and equipment. Even where costs are fully passed on in prices, more capital investment is required to produce a given amount of measured real GNP, so the economy does not grow as fast as the rate of investment in plant and equipment would appear to warrant. More capital is required to produce a constant increase in GNP, as it is measured, because GNP is incorrectly measured. In the past, the real costs of air and water pollution were ignored, so measured GNP was higher than actual GNP. Now that air and water pollution are being reduced, the resulting increase in actual GNP is not measured, and instead it appears that the economy is merely experiencing slower real growth and more inflation.

Although all industrial countries are involved in attempts to reduce environmental pollution through various forms of regulation, the current U.S. program is both more ambitious and more expensive than those that are under way in most other major OECD countries. Tables 4–8 and 4–9, which are based on an OECD study of environmental protection laws and on OECD forecasts of GNP and investment in the various countries, suggest two interesting conclusions. First, except for Japan, the costs of pollution control will apparently be a higher percentage of GNP and of the growth of GNP in the United States than in the other countries. Second, again except for Japan, the percentage of these costs that is to be borne by industry rather than by government is higher in the United States than elsewhere. Because the U.S. program is larger and more expensive and because a relatively high percentage of the costs are to be absorbed by industries (or their customers through price increases), pollution control laws have almost certainly had a much greater negative effect on investment that would add to productive capacity in the United States than elsewhere. In other words, additions to U.S. productive capacity are made more expensive by environmental laws, and a substantial part of the investment budgets of U.S. firms are needed to reequip preexisting plants to meet pollution requirements. If the costs of new capacity increase and if larger amounts of capital are required to clean up old plants without adding to capacity, it

---

7   This problem is well known by economists, and arises whenever the economic system exhibits major externalities, i.e., some spillover of a market process on a nonparticipant. Nobody decides to "purchase" pollution, but all neighbors of some types of factories get it anyway.

would hardly be surprising if U.S. firms are discouraged from making new investments. It makes more sense for firms to hire more labor to run existing plants more intensively than to build new facilities.

Except for Japan, where air and water pollution problems are particularly severe, the environmental protection programs of other major OECD countries do not appear to impose such burdens on private firms or their customers. As a result, the negative impact on capacity-creating plant and equipment investment should be considerably smaller.

Environmental protection is not the only area in which recent regulatory changes have imposed large costs on U.S. industries that might be expected to

TABLE 4-8. TOTAL EXPENDITURE ON NEW PROGRAMS OF
POLLUTION CONTROL AFTER ADJUSTMENTS AS
(1) A PERCENTAGE OF TOTAL GNP OVER THE
PROGRAM PERIOD, AND (2) A PERCENTAGE OF THE
GROWTH IN TOTAL GNP OVER THE PROGRAM
PERIOD

	New Program Total Expenditure	New Program Total Expenditure
	Percentage of Total GNP	Percentage of Total Growth of GNP
A. 1971–75		
U.S.	0.8	7.0
Italy	0.4	3.0
Japan[a]	3.0–5.5	11.1–20.6
Netherlands	0.04	3.8
Sweden[a]	0.5–0.9	4.9–9.0
W. Ger.	0.8	6.0
B. 1976–80		
U.S.	1.7	13.5
Italy	1.3	7.5
Netherlands	1.3	10.6
C. 1971–80		
U.S.	1.4	7.0
Italy	0.9	3.0
Netherlands	0.9	7.6
U.K.[a,b]	0.3–0.5	1.3–2.6

[a]These numbers have been adjusted upward to allow for operating costs on the basis of the relation between operating costs and investment in other countries.

[b]Adjusted upward by 15 percent to allow for solid waste disposal.
Source: OECD Studies in Resource Allocation, *Economic Implications of Pollution Control: A General Assessment* (February 1974), p. 30.
Reprinted with permission.

**TABLE 4-9. GOVERNMENT AND INDUSTRIAL EXPENDITURE
ON POLLUTION CONTROL**

	Government Sector	Industry Sector	Non-allocatable	Total
	In Percent of Total			
U.S.				
Total expenditure	15.6	70.1	14.3	100.0
of which: Air	3.3	57.2	—	56.0
Water	12.3	17.4	—	29.7
Solid waste	—	—	14.3	14.3
Investment	19.3	78.2	2.5	100.0
of which: Air	1.1	56.3	—	57.4
Water	18.2	21.9	—	40.1
Solid waste	—	—	2.5	2.5
Japan*				
Investment	20.7	79.3	—	100.0
Sweden				
Investment	73.0	27.0	—	100.0
West Germany				
Investment	43.9	55.4	—	100.0

*The Japanese Social and Economic Plan for 1973–77 indicates a marked change in the relationship to 45 percent for the government sector and 55 percent for the industry sector for that period.
Source: OECD Studies in Resource Allocation, *Economic Implications of Pollution Control: A General Assessment* (February 1974), p. 48.
Reprinted with permission.

discourage new investment. The Occupational Safety and Health Act and related measures dealing with safety in mining have sharply increased the costs of running many industries. In this case, as with pollution abatement, society as a whole probably benefits but the private investor does not. The extreme detail of the OSHA regulations makes it quite doubtful, however, that society's benefits justify what are often striking increases in costs. In any event, this is another case in which social and private benefits differ and in which large costs are imposed on private firms in order to gain what are hoped to be large social benefits. Such private costs either reduce the profitability of capacity-creating investments, lead to more inflation as the costs are passed on in prices, or some combination of the two. However the costs are borne, no increases in measured GNP occur because of the way GNP is measured. The real costs to society of occupational injuries and deaths were largely ignored in GNP figures in the past, so when these costs are reduced through OSHA regulations, no increase in GNP is registered.

Edward Denison recently completed a study of the effects of pollution control and OSHA requirements on measures of U.S. GNP. He concluded that U.S. GNP in 1975 was 1 percent lower because of recent pollution control laws and 0.4 percent lower because of safety and health regulations.[8] If the benefits to society resulting from a cleaner environment and fewer occupational injuries were fully reflected in GNP data, the net losses would have been considerably smaller.

PERCEIVED INVESTOR RISKS

Investments in new plant and equipment (or financial investments in common stock which finance such real investments) are made in response to expected yields *after* allowance for risk—that is, for the probability of unforeseen events which would reduce or eliminate those yields. When perceived risks increase, expected yields must be higher to attrack a given volume of investment.

For a number of reasons, perceived risks in making plant and equipment investments have almost certainly increased in the United States in recent years and have probably increased in the other major OECD economies. Evidence of such perceived risks can be found in the behavior of the U.S. stock market. Common stocks used to sell for 15 or 20 times earnings, which implied an ultimate yield of 5 to 7 percent, only slightly above corporate bond yields existing then. These same equities sold for less than 7 times earnings in mid-1979, which implied a yield of over 14 percent, well above corporate bond yields at that time. Investors apparently view the future profitability of major U.S. firms as being far less certain than in the past, and this increased risk is reflected in the low multiples of current earnings that they are willing to pay for equities, and in the fact that they are often willing to pay less than book value for what appear to be sound and profitable firms.

One likely reason for the increases in perceived risk in making investments in the United States is regulatory instability. The vast increase in federal and state regulations of business has involved large numbers of separate government entities and has been largely uncoordinated. The result has been a blizzard of poorly thought out, unforeseen and often conflicting regulatory actions. These regulations change frequently as office holders or political goals change, and investors are left in great uncertainty as to how a new project might be affected by future regulatory shifts. The Environmental Protection Agency tells firms to switch from coal to oil to reduce air pollution; the Department of Energy tells the same firms to switch from oil to coal to reduce oil imports. EPA says fine, but it must be low sulphur coal, yet such coal is not readily available. The federal government tells oil companies to find a cheap way to ship North Slope oil to the Midwest, but the state of California creates impossible regulatory barriers to the construction of a pipeline that is the obvious answer to the shipping problem. There seem to be more federal and state agencies regulating business than can be counted, and there is an obvious lack of coordination among them. The result is a constantly changing and chaotic regulatory environment in which many companies have no way of knowing whether a new facility will be allowed to operate if it is built, or whether expensive modifications will be required before operation. The process of getting construction and other permits in many environmentally sensitive industries is so long and

---

8   Edward Denison, "Effect of Selected Changes in the Institutional and Human Environment upon Output Per Unit of Input," *Survey of Current Business* (January 1978), p. 2144.

TABLE 4-10.   RELATIVE RATES OF U.S. INFLATION
(Average Annual Percent Change)

Index	1947–59	1959–69	1969–79
Farm products	– 1.1%	1.1%	7.5%
Fuels	2.5	1.5	16.4
Other raw materials	2.0	0.8	9.3
Lumber	2.9	2.4	8.3
Machinery	4.2	1.6	6.5
Wholesale prices	1.8	1.2	7.5
Consumer prices	2.2	2.3	6.4
Compensation per manhour	5.4	5.0	6.6
GNP deflator	2.3	2.5	6.5

Source: *Economic Report of the President, 1979,* pp. 206, 244, 259, and 265–266.

involved that a firm can spend many millions of dollars before it even knows whether construction will be possible.

The rational response to the additional risks and costs created by this regulatory maze is to pursue only those investment projects for which expected profit rates are particularly high. Projects which would have been undertaken in a less confused and uncertain regulatory environment are abandoned, and the total volume of plant and equipment investment is reduced.

Sharp and unforeseen changes in relative prices within the U.S. economy have recently added a new element of risk and uncertainty for investments in plant and equipment. As can be seen in Table 4-10, agricultural and other raw materials prices rose less rapidly than either the consumer price index or the GNP deflator during the 1947–69 period, but except for agriculture, the differences were modest. During the 1970s, however, the prices of primary products rose much more rapidly than either the broad price index or average employee compensation.

These rapid shifts in relative prices have redistributed income away from the urban sector of the economy as a whole, consumers at large, and those parts of the business sector which produce goods and services other than raw materials. Agriculture and forestry and firms producing a variety of other raw materials have benefited. The uneven nature of recent inflation produces a new and large element of risk in the economy.

Investments in new plant and equipment in the primary projects sector have recently been more profitable than such investments elsewhere in the economy. To the extent that these differing rates of inflation accurately reflect underlying relative scarcities in the economy, this pattern of profits should act as a signal for increasing future investments in facilities to produce raw materials and is consequently desirable. During the 1970s, however, investment responses to these signals have been relatively slow, in part due to the uncertainty associated with rapid general rates of inflation and the regulatory environment. It is far from certain that these relative scarcities are more than transitory, and hence that recent patterns of price changes will continue. If this price pattern were reversed during the 1980s, current investments in primary products capacity will not be profitable, and there is no way for firms to know whether the pattern of the 1970s will be maintained or reversed. It is clear, however, that the earlier pattern in which prices in almost all sectors of the economy except agriculture rose at about the same rate has ended, and that the recent differences in relative price movements have created a new element of uncertainty for those planning investments in plant and equipment throughout the economy. Such increases in perceived risks tend to discourage investments in new plant and equipment.

Other Factors: Technology and the Terms of Trade 5

TECHNOLOGICAL CHANGE: R&D AS A FORM OF INVESTMENT

Technological advances which increase the productivity of capital and labor are the result of a combination of R&D expenditures, other innovative activities, and luck. Spending money on research and development is analogous to drilling for oil. A firm invests resources where it thinks profitable possibilities exist, but there is a large element of risk or luck in whether anything useful is actually discovered. The easy oil is found first, just as the easy inventions of technological breakthroughs are developed first, so both drilling for oil and maintaining a productive R&D program with a given science base should become more expensive as time passes. As less likely geological prospects are drilled and as more difficult scientific problems are investigated, the cost of producing extra barrels of oil and additional cost reductions through technological gains increase.

The forces behind private R&D expenditures are very similar to those behind plant and equipment expenditures. Both involve committing funds now in expectation of recovering them profitably later. Both are encouraged by higher expected future profit rates and discouraged by the higher cost of borrowing or otherwise raising funds for current expenditures. The element of risk in R&D expenditures, however, is higher. If a factory is not successful, it can usually be sold to someone else for at least a partial recovery of the initial investment. An R&D project that fails to produce a marketable product or a way to reduce the costs of producing an old product is worthless. There is no physical asset to sell and the expenditure is a complete loss.

The fact that R&D expenditures are viewed as a current cost provides a somewhat more favorable taxation climate than exists for plant and equipment investments, which can only be amortized over a number of years. A firm can recover 46 percent (the federal corporate tax rate) of an R&D expenditure immediately through lower corporate profits taxes, but the same recovery takes many years for an expenditure on new plant and equipment.

Another advantage in R&D investments is that technological knowledge is a kind of intangible capital which can be used over and over at no additional cost. Once the investment is made and a new product or process is successfully developed, little or no further R&D investment is needed no matter how often the process is used or how many units of the new product are produced. A doubling of the physical capacity to produce a product typically requires an approximate doubling of investment in plant and equipment, but no further investment in research and development. As a result, there are large economies of scale in the application of technological developments.

Publicly funded research expenditures also represent a current investment in hope of future returns and also involve large elements of risk. The main difference is that the resulting technical knowledge has elements of a public good in that it benefits society at large rather than particular private investors. If the research is outside of the classified defense area, the resulting knowledge is typically made available to the public (including potential foreign users) at no cost. If the research is in the classified defense area, the results are obviously not made public, but presumably do meet broad social needs for an effective defense force. In that case, there may be private spillover benefits for the firm doing the research under government contract if it can find nonsensitive ways to use some of the new technology in a nonmilitary product or process. The rather close similarity between the original Boeing 707 and an airplane which Boeing had previously developed and produced for the air force is an example of such a spillover.

RECENT U.S. R&D EXPERIENCE

Another cause of the disappointing performance of U.S. labor productivity growth can be found in the evidence on U.S. R&D expenditures.

Table 5–1 shows that the percentage of U.S. GNP spent on research and development declined during a period in which it increased in a number of other major competitive economies. The U.S. economy is so large, however, that it still outspends other countries on research and development in absolute terms by a large margin, but the margin is not as large as it was in the 1960s.

Figure 5–1 illustrates a sizable shift away from government-financed R&D expenditures in the United States and a modest increase in private efforts. Since the public (particularly federal) sector is typically more interested in defense and pure scientific research and less interested in short-term applications than is the private sector, this decline in public funding implies a shift toward short-run applied research and away from long-term effects. This suggests trouble in the future as

TABLE 5-1. RESEARCH AND DEVELOPMENT EXPENDITURES AS A PERCENTAGE OF GNP, SELECTED YEARS

	1963	1973	1976	1978
U.S.	2.9%	2.3%	2.3%	2.3%
Canada	0.9	0.9	1.1[a]	NA
France	1.6	1.8	1.8	1.8[c]
Japan	1.4	1.9	1.9	NA
U.K.	2.3	1.9	2.1[b]	NA
USSR	2.8	3.7	3.6	3.5[c]
West Germany	1.4	2.3	2.3	2.3

[a] 1974.

[b] 1975.

[c] 1977.

Sources: *National Science Board, Science Indicators*, 1974, 1976, 1978; U.S., *International Economic Report of the President, 1978.*

FIGURE 5–1. R&D EXPENDITURES, CONSTANT PRICES, 1973 = 100

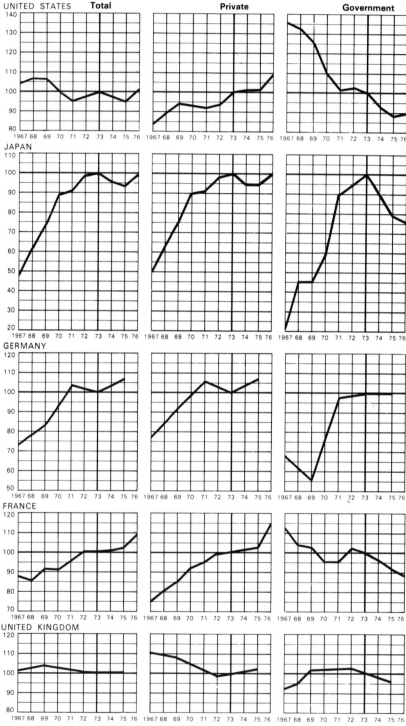

Source: *OECD Observer* (March 1979), p. 14. Reproduced with permission.

basic scientific breakthroughs slow down and the practical application of those breakthroughs become less frequent. A shift away from basic science may not have striking effects on new products and processes in the short run, but it certainly will over a period of time.

The results of R&D efforts can be seen in the number of U.S. inventions patented abroad relative to the number of foreign inventions patented in the United States. The higher the "patent balance," the stronger the U.S. research effort relative to other countries. Table 5-2 shows that the U.S. patent balance has declined since the 1960s.

Although these figures are only a rough indicator of research results because the patented products or processes vary widely in their economic value and because many new inventions are not patented, the trend is fairly clear. The U.S. position worldwide remains very strong, but it is not as strong as it was in the 1960s.

The United States remains the largest source of R&D effort and technological output, but its lead has clearly narrowed in recent years, and the United States is behind in some important specific product areas, such as cameras and some consumer electronics.

Part of this decline is almost certainly a natural process of European and Japanese recovery from the effects of World War II. Science and technology were very strong in Europe before World War II, and the postwar U.S. dominance was an unusual and temporary situation resulting from the war's destruction. Germany has always been a leader in many areas of science, and it is not surprising to see German firms regain their position in chemicals and many areas of engineering. The U.S. decline is, however, also the result of a declining U.S. R&D effort and ought to be disturbing, particularly if the decline is clearest in basic scientific research which has large long-term impacts and where rapid recovery is not possible.

The reduction of public funding for research began with the severe budgetary pressures in the Vietnam era. Massive military expenditures, without offsetting tax increases, made it necessary to reduce expenditures somewhere, and research and development was one area. Vietnam expenditures were replaced in the 1970s by a

TABLE 5-2. U.S. PATENT BALANCE, 1966-75[a]

	1966	1970	1973	1975
Worldwide	36,066	33,697	25,306	19,197
With:				
Canada	15,676	17,598	11,619	10,891
Japan	3,561	2,149	546	− 1,421
U.K.	11,440	9,776	8,866	8,436
West Germany	− 248	− 1,152	− 639	− 2,929
Other EC countries[b]	5,700	5,743	4,914	4,372
USSR	− 63	− 17	− 177	− 152

[a]Foreign patents to U.S. nationals less U.S. patents to foreign nationals.

[b]Excluding France.

Source: NSF, *Science Indicators*, 1974 and 1976.

tremendous increase in transfer payments, with the same results. Cutting research programs became a way to reduce expenditures to make room for a variety of social welfare program expansions without increases in tax rates. The space program, which generated substantial private-sector spinoffs, was particularly hard hit during this period of retrenchment.

The decline in federal funding of research is also the result of sharp reductions in new military weapons programs, which have been a major source of past research efforts, and of a declining political interest in supporting post-secondary education. Federal expenditures aimed at universities and colleges grew rapidly in the late 1950s and early '60s in response to both the Sputnik challenge and the arrival of the baby boom at college age. Both of these events have passed, and public interest in universities and colleges has declined. The campus riots of the early 1970s and some other aspects of student behavior in the counterculture era may have encouraged this decline. The number of college-age students is now falling, and support of universities and colleges is no longer an important political priority. Since most pure or basic scientific research is done in university laboratories, a decline in support of these institutions necessarily implies a decline in such research. If the major universities face a financially difficult decade during the 1980s, as is widely predicted, basic science research will probably suffer further. If public financing of research remains low in a period of rapidly declining student enrollments, university laboratories will be in deep trouble.

Private research efforts by corporations are affected by the same forces that affect plant and equipment expenditures. The cost of raising funds has increased sharply and some of the perceived risks have gotten worse. The rapid increase in federal and state regulations of business activity has made it much more difficult to introduce many types of new products. The procedures of the Food and Drug Administration have become so lengthy and expensive as to inhibit pharmaceutical research and make it almost impossible to undertake for all but the largest and strongest firms. Other OECD countries have considerably shorter and less bureaucratic procedures, and as a result, new drugs are introduced abroad much more rapidly than in the United States. Similar problems have been created in other areas by the growing activity of the Consumer Product Safety Council. Burgeoning regulatory measures discourage research efforts through the economy, but are particularly hard on small firms with limited capital. Large and established firms have sufficient capital and legal manpower to continue to operate successfully whereas small high technology firms may not.

THE TERMS OF TRADE AND REAL INCOMES

The amount of real income which participants in an economy receive from their output depends in part on the relationship between the economy's export and import prices. The higher that ratio is, the greater the volume of imports an economy can purchase and consume with the revenue earned from a constant quantity of exports. Shifts in the ratio of export to import prices (the terms of trade) can produce large movements in real incomes in economies that are heavily dependent on international trade. Even in countries such as the United States, where international trade represents a smaller part of GNP, sharp increases in the prices of imports can reduce real incomes significantly.

Table 5-3 shows that during the 1960s, the terms of trade improved for the United States, the United Kingdom, Germany, and France, but declined substantially for Japan and moderately for Canada. Since the 1968-70 period, however, the terms of trade declined substantially for the United States (23.2 percent), the United Kingdom (9.4 percent) and Japan (14.7 percent). Over the same period, Canada's terms of trade improved 2.2 percent, in part because it was not a large net energy importer. Germany's terms of trade improved 7.4 percent and France's declined only 1.0 percent during this period partly because of its better-defined energy policies.

The worsening of the U.S. terms of trade during the 1970s was not the dominant factor in the poor performance of the U.S. economy, but it certainly was a significant element. Imports represent about 9.5 percent of U.S. GNP, so the 23.2 percent deterioration of the U.S. terms of trade during the 1969-78 period implies a reduction of 2.20 percent in U.S. real incomes, that is, if the U.S. terms of trade had not deteriorated since 1972, Americans would be able to consume and otherwise use 2.20 percent more goods and services on the basis of the same level of output. 2.20 percent may not seem like much, but it represents almost a full year's real GNP growth at rates prevailing during the mid-1970s.

TABLE 5-3. TERMS OF TRADE USING INDEXES (1975 = 1.00) OF UNIT VALUES IN TERMS OF U.S. DOLLARS, 1960-78

	U.S.	Canada	France	Japan	U.K.	W. Ger.
1960	1.15	0.92	0.93	1.50	1.12	0.89
1961	1.21	0.90	0.96	1.42	1.15	0.89
1962	1.24	0.88	1.00	1.38	1.17	0.93
1963	1.21	0.87	0.98	1.32	1.17	0.96
1964	1.18	0.85	1.00	1.32	1.16	0.96
1965	1.23	0.87	1.00	1.23	1.19	0.94
1966	1.22	0.89	1.02	1.23	1.20	0.94
1967	1.21	0.91	1.00	1.28	1.20	0.94
1968	1.24	0.91	1.02	1.32	1.16	0.94
1969	1.26	0.90	1.04	1.37	1.16	0.94
1970	1.24	0.92	1.02	1.38	1.20	0.98
1971	1.20	0.91	1.04	1.36	1.20	1.02
1972	1.15	0.91	1.05	1.42	1.21	1.05
1973	1.13	0.97	1.07	1.37	1.08	1.01
1974	0.96	1.04	0.92	1.08	0.91	0.94
1975	1.00	1.00	1.00	1.00	1.00	1.00
1976	1.01	1.03	0.99	0.96	0.99	0.99
1977	0.96	0.97	0.97	1.06	1.01	0.98
1978	0.96	0.93	1.02	1.16	1.06	1.02
Percentage change 1968, '69 and '70 Average to 1978	− 23.2%	+ 2.2%	− 1.0%	− 14.7%	− 9.4%	+ 7.4%

Source: IMF, *International Financial Statistics*, lines 74 and 75.

The deterioration of the U.S. terms of trade has had additional negative impacts on the economy as various organized groups in society have tried to recapture this real income loss through indexing, cost-of-living allowances and similar techniques. Real incomes of Americans must decline if the country's terms of trade worsen and if everyone tries to avoid such reductions the result is merely a cost-push inflationary cycle. OPEC oil price increases raise the U.S. consumer price index, and unionized workers with cost-of-living clauses in their contracts receive offsetting pay increases, which are quickly passed through as price increases by their employers. The increase in the CPI triggers parallel increases in social security payments, which then require increases in payroll taxes. This causes increases in labor costs, which cause further price increases, and so on. As an economy increasingly indexes wage rates and transfer payments in an attempt to protect various groups from the possibility of real income losses, any significant worsening of the terms of trade through import price increases, which must reduce real incomes, sets off an inflationary process that can be far worse than the original terms of trade loss.

The sharp increase in the price of oil and some other raw materials, which caused the deterioration of the U.S. terms of trade, also had other purely internal effects on the U.S. economy. These price increases shift large amounts of income from consumers as a group to domestic owners of oil wells and some other raw materials supplies. The tremendous increase in energy prices has made a large part of the U.S. fixed capital stock, which was put in place when energy was cheap, obsolete or at least extremely expensive to operate. Although some groups have gained, much larger groups have lost, and both individuals and firms find themselves with fixed capital in the form of buildings and equipment that is no longer economically rational. Individuals have money invested in cars that use too much gas and houses that use too much heating oil, and the real income which they derive from the use of this capital falls. Firms have factories and machinery that use far too much energy and which are less profitable as a result. The great uncertainty about future energy prices makes it difficult to plan future investments in cars, houses, factories, and machinery with any assurance that they will be economical in 5 or 10 years.

Conclusions and Policy Options 6

The previous chapters have suggested several reasons for the unsatisfactory performance of the U.S. economy during recent years. Although increases in the prices of oil and other resources have undoubtedly contributed to the difficulties of the U.S. economy, the core of the problem is that the United States saves and invests a far smaller percentage of GNP than most of its major OECD competitors. Americans consume a larger share of what they produce than their trading partners. As a result, the U.S. stock of productive capital grows slowly and is far older and less technologically current than the capital stocks in Japan and various European countries. If R&D activities and technological advance represent an important form of "investment," another area of declining U.S. investment becomes apparent. The percentage of GNP spent on such activities has been falling in the United States while it has been rising elsewhere.

GOVERNMENT POLICIES AS A CAUSE OF SLOW GROWTH

Behind the low rates of saving and investment in the United States lie a series of government policies which have been strongly oriented toward goals other than economic growth. The tax system has put great emphasis on "equity" at the cost of discouraging activities which contribute to economic growth of the kind that generates higher average real income. Profits are taxed both at the corporate level and at the personal level (when dividends are received), discouraging investment in common stocks. Taxation of capital gains became much heavier in the 1970s, with the same effect, although this change in tax laws has now been largely reversed. Interest income of individuals is fully taxed even when it is less than sufficient to offset the effects of inflation on past savings, leaving people generally with negative aftertax real interest rates. The tax system has provided an increasing disincentive for personal saving.

Social welfare and transfer-payments systems have been expanded rapidly, not only to protect many Americans against the possibility of erosion of their real incomes, but also to extend the role of the government in meeting many perceived financial needs. Since provision for the possibility of a "rainy day" is a major reason for personal saving, the constant expansion of such programs has the unfortunate side effect of further reducing personal savings rates.

Because the rapid increases in federal transfer payments (and the previous expenditures for Vietnam) were not fully financed with parallel increases in tax rates, there has been a large increase in the size of annual federal deficits. These deficits now occur at *all* stages of the business cycle and constitute a major source of dissaving, which limits investment. The private sector saves but the federal government dissaves, leaving a persistent shortage of total saving in the economy.

The result is that resources are simply not available for the levels of investment that are required for a high rate of basic economic growth.[1]

Government policies have also produced a massive increase in public regulation of business. Environmental protection, occupational health and safety, equal-opportunity employment, and numerous other programs have imposed large and often unforeseen costs on the regulated industries. Since these regulations have been changing constantly, and since the federal and state regulatory process has become increasingly complex and difficult to understand, major additional risks as well as higher costs have been created for firms considering new projects, thus discouraging new plant and equipment-sum investments.

All of these government policies reflect important social and political values. Voters, or at least their elected representatives, have supported changes in the tax system that are purported to make it more "equitable." The environment was being debased and needed attention, too many jobs were unsafe or unhealthy, and many people were financially unprepared for large medical costs, retirement or other financially demanding situations. The problem is not the desirable goal of eliminating or reducing these and other deficiencies, but the fact that the particular government policies chosen to deal with them have had large and generally unforeseen negative effects on the economy. As implemented, most of these policies discourage economic growth, and the effects are all on the supply side of the economy. Most critically, saving and investment, which would increase the capacity of the economy to produce goods and services, are discouraged.[2] R&D activity, another form of investment and thereby a source of resources for reducing social and environmental ills, is also discouraged.

FASTER ECONOMIC GROWTH: A POLITICAL CHOICE

The question now is whether economic growth should again become a major national priority and, if so, how such growth might be pursued. The voters may decide, of course, that economic growth should remain a secondary priority and that the goals of the last 15 years should be pursued with no major changes. When the growth of the U.S. labor force slows dramatically in the mid-1980s, however, the implications of little or no labor productivity increase will become even more stark. Some improvements in real GNP per capita have been possible in recent years despite very poor labor productivity performance because of the large increase in the participation rate and hence in the labor force, which means an increase in the ratio of income earners to the nonworking population. Such economic growth will not be possible in a few years, and the lack of labor productivity growth will then

---

1   The state and local government sector has been running a surplus during recent years. The public sector as a whole, however, was in deficit during 11 of the 14 years from 1966 through 1979. The total deficit for the 14 years was $144 billion (*Economic Report of the President, 1980*, p. 288). A large part of the recent state and local surplus has been in California, but Proposition 13 and the likely passage of another tax limitation measure will probably eliminate that state as a source of public saving.

2   For a fuller explanation of these negative-sum effects, see Theodore Geiger, *Welfare and Efficiency: Their Interactions in Western Europe and Implications for International Economic Relations* (Washington, D.C.. National Planning Association, 1978).

mean little or no increase in real per capita GNP. This lack will become particularly unpleasant when the number of retired Americans starts to expand rapidly in a few years. The growth, or perhaps even the level, of real income for the retired will have to be reduced if significant decreases in the rate of real income growth for the currently employed are to be avoided. This unpleasant choice can be avoided only if labor productivity and consequently real output per capita grow rapidly.

The option of significantly redesigning government policies to increase the rate of growth of the economy's productive capacity deserves attention. The following pages will suggest policies that might be expected to produce more rapid growth of U.S. productive capacity if a political decision were made to move in that direction. These policies, like those directed at earlier goals, will not be "free." They will require some temporary compromises in the pursuit of other major goals. One of the lessons of the last 15 years ought to be that the United States cannot do everything at the same time.

POLICY OPTIONS: THE SUPPLY SIDE

The evidence indicates that the lack of rapid economic growth in the United States during recent years has not resulted from insufficient levels of aggregate demand but, instead, from low rates of growth of productive capacity or potential supply. Therefore, the goal of the policies suggested here is to increase the capacity of the economy to produce. The options are all supply-side in that they are designed to add to the supply of goods and services rather than to raise the demand for them.

The most important single goal of these policy changes is to increase the percentage of GNP invested in plant and equipment. This is needed to increase both the capital/labor ratio, and hence labor productivity with given technology, and the rate at which new technology becomes embodied in new plant and equipment, and hence becomes useful. A high rate of investment in new plant and equipment means a higher capital/labor ratio and a younger capital stock that uses newer and more productive technology.

Increasing the percentage of GNP invested in plant and equipment unfortunately requires a reduction in the proportion of total output used for consumption. If the economy were operating at or close to full capacity, this would necessitate a reduction in the absolute volume of consumption (private or public), which would be politically difficult at best. It now seems very likely, however, that the U.S. economy will be passing through a recession by 1981 and, consequently, that considerable excess capacity will exist in many industries at the time when a decision might be made to adopt policies designed to increase significantly the economy's long-term rate of growth. If policies encouraging an increase in the percentage of GNP invested in plant and equipment were adopted during such a recession, a further decline in the volume of private or public consumption levels would not be necessary to create excess capacity in the economy that can be used to increase productive investment.[3] As the economy recovers from the recession,

---

3   If the recession is severe enough to require a tax cut to reflate the economy, the resulting changes in tax rates should be designed to encourage current investment in plant and equipment rather than a return to the consumption boom of the late 1970s.

however, the growth of consumption will have to be restrained in order to maintain levels of investment that are needed to produce an acceleration of long-term growth. If private and public consumption are allowed to grow as rapidly during the next recovery as they did during the last two upturns (1972–73 and 1976–78), resources will not remain available for the levels of plant and equipment investment required to maintain rapid growth.

INCREASED SAVINGS RATES: A NECESSITY FOR INVESTMENT GROWTH

The long-term increase in the savings rate, which is necessary to finance increased investment, can occur either in the private or the public (government) sector or both. Within the private sector, savings can occur either in households or in the form of retained earnings in businesses. In either case, the increase must be in real terms, that is, after allowance for inflation. Retained earnings have increased as a percentage of GNP and are now well over half of corporate profits, so further increases in savings from that sector are likely to be modest unless profits rise sharply as a percentage of GNP, or stockholders accept the idea that their dividends should not grow or perhaps not even keep up with inflation. Since both seem unlikely, increases in private savings will probably have to come primarily from households. Personal savings are a far lower proportion of income in the United States than in most other OECD countries and are now lower than they were in the past, so sizable increases in household savings ought to be possible. If Americans were to save as high a percentage of their income as the French, Germans or Canadians, a considerably higher level of productive investment would be possible without increased inflationary pressures.

The first goal of U.S. policy in this area should be to increase the rewards for saving, which means a permanent return to positive real aftertax interest rates. A sharp reduction in the rate of inflation would greatly encourage higher savings rates since it would end the recent situation in which long-term bonds have produced negative real yields even before taxes were paid on the interest income. A return to rates of inflation in the range of 4 to 5 percent would mean that corporate bonds bearing 10 percent nominal yields would produce positive pretax interest rates. Americans obviously do not have much incentive to save, rather than consume, if they are offered a real yield of minus 3 percent on such bonds before taxes are paid and a much larger negative yield after taxes.

Since it is very unlikely that inflation will decelerate in the near future to the 4 to 5 percent range of the 1960s, the tax system should be changed to allow for the difference between nominal and real interest income, and to tax only the latter. If the rate of inflation is 8 percent, a nominal interest rate of 8 percent is necessary merely to maintain the original capital and is not really income to the bond holder. It is both unfair and undesirable in terms of its effect on savings to tax such an interest payment. Taxes should be applied only to interest income which is in excess of that necessary to maintain the original capital. If the inflation rate were 6 percent and corporate bonds were yielding 9 percent, taxes should be applied to the real interest rate of 3 percent.

Such a tax reform would require investors to use the original purchase price of their bonds to calculate their losses of capital due to inflation each year. This loss would then be deducted from their interest income for tax purposes. As an alternative, the government could estimate the average interest rates earned in the United States during a year, divide that figure into the rate of inflation, and allow taxpayers to deduct that percentage of their interest income from taxable income. If, for example, the average interest rate were 10 percent and inflation were 6 percent, people would pay taxes on 40 percent of their interest income. This would represent a modest complication of the forms, but would both be fairer than the current system, which taxes unreal income, and act as an encouragement to increase saving.

Saving would also be encouraged by the repeal of Regulation Q. Under present conditions, those who hold savings or checking accounts are limited by law to absurdly low interest rates. Regulation Q was designed to help the housing industry by providing a flow of low-cost funds into thrift institutions which make mortgage loans. It provides this help by discriminating against savers who deposit funds in such institutions. Recent changes in the regulations allow higher interest rates on large deposit certificates or on more modest amounts deposited for 30 months. This represents a considerable improvement, but is still unfair to small savers who do not have access to the large certificates and who cannot afford to commit funds for such a long period. Regulation Q should be abandoned and interest rates on all forms of bank deposits, including checking accounts, should be determined by market forces. If the government wants to subsidize the housing industry, it could do so without requiring that small savers accept unfairly low interest rates. In order to protect savings banks and other thrift institutions from large losses on outstanding mortgages which bear low interest rates, Regulation Q should be removed over a period of time by raising the ceiling on interest rates by a modest amount each year until it ceases to restrain market yields. In the meantime, the majority of the old mortgages with low interest rates would have been paid off or reduced in size to a level at which they represent little or no financial threat to savings institutions. If Regulation Q is removed quickly, modest federal aid may be appropriate to help cover financial institution losses on old mortgages with low interest rates.[3a]

If interest rates on time deposits were to increase due to the repeal of Regulation Q, the Treasury would undoubtedly find it very difficult to sell savings bonds at the low interest rates which they now offer. Yields on savings bonds would have to be increased if they were to remain competitive. More attractive interest rates on these bonds might also encourage a modest increase in the overall savings rates.

Households save in part as a precaution against unforeseen future needs. If a social welfare system protected all people fully against all such financially demanding occurrences, it would discourage personal savings. This would suggest that the social security system and any future national health insurance system should not be run in a way that removes *all* need for savings for old age or medical expenses on the part of people during their years of gainful employment. A universal and compulsory health insurance program covering all medical costs, for example, would clearly eliminate one major reason for personal savings by people

---

3a   While this study was in the process of being printed, Congress passed and President Carter signed a bill eliminating Regulation Q over a period of years.

economically able to save. A system of national insurance against catastrophic medical costs, however, would not eliminate the need for saving, and should be considered as an alternative to the more comprehensive approach for that reason. Social insurance programs should be designed to protect people against financial needs which prudent people cannot be expected to handle, but not to encourage a complete lack of saving for unforeseen needs. If society provides complete protection against virtually all personal financial emergencies regardless of income or need, it should not be surprised if people fail to plan for such possibilities and neglect to save.

The possibility of leaving wealth to one's heirs constitutes another reason for saving, particularly late in life. Inheritance taxes which are extremely high then become a strong disincentive for saving and an incentive for dissaving among relatively wealthy elderly people. If such taxes are high enough, people have no reason whatever to conserve their resources in their later years and are instead encouraged to turn their net worth into annuities, the full proceeds of which are spent before death. With the elderly constituting a large and growing proportion of a stable population, dissaving in this group could fully offset saving among those who are younger, producing a zero savings rate for society as a whole. Saving, or at least the avoidance of dissaving, is encouraged among the elderly only if a sizable proportion of their resources can be passed on to the next generation. Proponents of "tax reform" sometimes suggest considerably higher inheritance taxes as a way of encouraging social and economic mobility within society. The practical effect of such high inheritance taxes would be to encourage massive dissaving among the elderly. Tax reforms which would produce this result should be avoided as counterproductive for society as a whole.

THE PUBLIC SECTOR AS A SOURCE OF SAVINGS OR OF LESS DISSAVINGS

The greatest opportunities for increasing savings rates are probably not in households but instead in the public sector. The federal government has become a massive source of dissaving during the last 15 years as it typically has run large budget deficits at all stages of the business cycle. Keynesian economics has often been blamed for the inflationary results, but it is a misreading of Keynes to suggest that his writings support such policies. He implied that budget deficits are to be run in recessions when new business investment is low and that a balanced budget or modest surplus is called for during strong cyclical recoveries. Those directing U.S. fiscal policy, however, have followed the first half of the policy but ignored the second. During fiscal 1978, when the U.S. economy was three years into a strong cyclical recovery, the federal deficit was about $28 billion. Allowing for off-budget items, such as the Export-Import Bank and other federal credit programs, the Treasury needed about $40 billion in new funds. A federal deficit of $28 billion when the economy is operating at close to full capacity and when inflation is rampant is not a countercyclical fiscal policy.

The economy's savings rate can be increased significantly if the federal government will return to an "orthodox" fiscal policy of running sizable deficits only during recessions and parallel surpluses during strong recoveries. Balancing the federal budget each year makes no sense because it would then be impossible to use fiscal policy to deal with real recessions; however, balancing the budget over the whole business cycle does make sense. Deficits during recessions would be offset by surpluses during booms, and the federal government would cease to be a source of dissaving over the long-run.

This shift in the budget should not be made suddenly. The role of the federal government in the economy is so large that a sudden substantial reduction in the cyclically adjusted or "full employment" budget deficit would be very disruptive. Estimates of the budget should be developed each year that indicate how large the deficit would be if the economy were at its average or normal level of capacity utilization. The budget measured on this basis should be moved toward balance over several years. The actual budget would still show sizable deficits during recessions when the economy was operating at less than average or normal capacity utilization. Surpluses would occur on the opposing side of the cycle, and the budget deficit over the whole business cycle would slowly decline over several years. At the end of this process, the budget would be in balance whenever the economy was at its average level of employment and capacity utilization.

Such a policy shift would require long-run budgetary planning by Congress and by the executive branch. It would also require a great deal of political fortitude because the normal growth of expenditures would have to be reduced somewhat or tax rates would have to be increased, neither of which is popular.

REFORMING SOCIAL SECURITY TO INCREASE SAVINGS

Changes in the social security system that would make it an actuarially sound pension program would do a great deal to move the budget toward long-run balance. In recent years, social security benefits have been increased at a rate well in excess of the growth of receipts, and the trust funds are now declining. This has occurred because Congress has run social security like a welfare program while claiming that it is a system of social insurance. Benefits have not been tied directly to what each participant and his or her employer contributed, and benefits have been extended to groups that have contributed little or nothing during their working lifetimes. Benefits were increased rapidly both for those who were in real need and for those who were not. Benefits were raised for the latter group on the argument that social security is an insurance program and, since these people paid their taxes earlier, they should now get benefits. But, the benefits were not based on what they had paid in and rapidly became far higher than their contributions warranted. An insurance program was confused with a welfare program, and the result was mounting deficits and potentially depleted trust funds.

This situation can be remedied by distinguishing between two public goals and by dealing with them separately. The social security system should be designed to provide retirement insurance for all workers on the principle that each participant receives benefits that are directly related to what he or she and the employer paid as premiums. At retirement, a monthly payment is calculated on the basis of these premiums and currently accurate actuarial tables. No benefit increases are provided later because the basis of the system is that people get out of it what they put in plus accumulated interest. The second and separate goal is to see that the elderly, as well as those in other age groups, have sufficient incomes to avoid real hardship. For retirees for whom social security plus private pensions and savings are inadequate, separate payments should be made based on clearly established need. These payments would not be made to retirees whose incomes are sufficient to avoid hardship, and it would be made clear that people are expected to prepare for their retirement years in part through private pensions and savings during their gainfully employed years.

Such a reform of the social security system would have two major advantages. First, the system would become a clear source of net savings as workers accumulated assets and pension rights during their working lifetimes and used those assets during retirement. Second, the federal budget would not be thrown into deficit in the future, when the size of the retired population will be rising, by automatic benefit increases both to those in need and to those who are relatively well off. An increasing number of retirees have sizable private pensions, and the current social security system provides automatic benefit increases to such people irrespective of need.[4] Federal expenditure increases could be considerably reduced by adopting a negative income tax system for the elderly that would provide payments beyond their funded social security premiums only for those in need.

These changes in the operation of the social security system are quite basic and would have sizable impacts on benefit payments in the years ahead to many who are currently retired or will be retiring in the future. In order to avoid unnecessary disruption and the complaint that it is unfair suddenly to change a system which is of such importance to the elderly, these reforms should be phased in over a considerable period of time. If the rate of automatic increase in benefits were reduced over a period as long as a decade or more, and if the availability of additional payments to the needy elderly were phased in at the same time, the desired changes in the system could be accomplished without unreasonable disruption for current beneficiaries. It would be important, however, that everyone understand at the beginning of the process just what changes were being made and that current members of the labor force be encouraged to plan for them.

Recent increases in longevity and the prospective decline in the number of new labor-force entrants mean that the ratio of retirees to active workers is going to increase sharply over the next few decades. If adequate social security benefits for the retired are to remain possible without sharp increases in payroll taxes, the age at which people become eligible to receive retirement benefits under the social security system will probably have to be raised above 65. If people are going to live four or five years longer than they did in the past, it does not seem unreasonable to expect that two or perhaps two and one-half additional years be spent in the labor force. Such an increase would mean two more years of saving in the form of additional payments into the social security system, which will provide a one-time increase in aggregate savings. Increases in the minimum retirement age for full social security benefits should be made in small increments (perhaps one or two months at a time) and should be timed to coincide with periods of cyclical strength in the economy to avoid sizable but temporary increases in the unemployment rate.

---

4   Federal costs for maintenance of the elderly could also be reduced if federal employees were included in the social security system. Federal pensions are currently based on the assumption that civil servants will not receive social security, but many public employees manage to accumulate just enough time in the private sector to qualify for social security, and then combine a generous (and fully indexed) public pension with social security benefits. The result is very high public costs for the retirement of such people.

POLICIES TO INCREASE PRODUCTIVE INVESTMENT

The policies described in the previous section are all intended to increase the U.S. economy's rate of saving. If they were adopted and had their intended effect, the flow of new funds into capital markets, which would be available for the financing of productive investment, would increase. This would cause interest rates to decline, which would encourage more investment. It is very unlikely, however, that the decreased costs of borrowing would be sufficient to produce enough additional investment to use all of the real resources made available by the reduced level of consumption. Other measures would be necessary to encourage investment if the additional saving is not to produce a decline in aggregate demand in the economy and the potential for a recession. The goal of policy initiatives should be to encourage an increase in productive investment that approximately matches the increase in savings when the economy is operating at the desired level of aggregate demand.

Changes in the tax structure are probably the most important single way of achieving these objectives. Personal and corporate income taxes should be integrated into a single tax on income from all sources. The current system of double taxation of corporate profits (corporate profits taxes and personal income taxes when dividends are paid) produces total tax rates on profits that discourage the provision of equity capital through the purchase of common stocks. The inability of new and relatively risky firms to raise equity funds is a particular problem which results in part from the tax environment.

The corporate profits tax should be abolished, and stockholders should be taxed on earnings per share rather than on dividends, with corporations withholding taxes on behalf of their stockholders. Since stockholders pay taxes on retained earnings as well as on dividends, their cost basis for the later calculation of capital gains must be increased by the amount of such retentions. A single tax on income would then be in effect, which could be more or less progressive as Congress wished, and income produced by corporate profits would not be taxed any differently than income from other sources. Capital gains should then be indexed for inflation in order to tax real rather than nominal gains and would thus be treated as regular income. Capital losses (also indexed) would be treated symmetrically and would hence be deducted from income.

The revenue lost by the integration of corporate and personal income taxes could be recovered through taxes on consumption, such as a value-added tax.[5] The result of these reforms would be to create a single tax on all income which did not discriminate against profits as a source of income. This would encourage the provision of equity or risk capital by savers, making it far easier to finance plant and equipment investment in new or risky firms that cannot borrow readily. Such a change in the tax system would also shift the burden of taxes from production to consumption, encouraging the former and discouraging the latter.

---

5   The value-added tax is far from a perfect solution to the problem of how to recover revenues lost through the integration of personal and corporate income taxes, but it does have the advantage of representing a tax on consumption rather than production or savings. If a proportional tax on consumption is felt to be unacceptably regressive, food might be exempted. Since a value-added tax can be rebated on exports and collected as a border tax on imports, it ought to be popular with U.S. exporters and import competitors.

Changes in depreciation schedules provide another opportunity to encourage new capital formation. The current schedules require much longer write-off periods than those in most other major OECD countries. Companies are encouraged to maintain old buildings and machinery because so long a period is required to recover the original investment as depreciation. Accelerated depreciation schedules would reduce the tax liability facing a firm (or the stockholder if the previously described changes occurred) if it had recently invested in new plant and equipment. Once the depreciation period was over, however, the firm's tax liability would rise and its cash flow would decline unless it made further investments in new buildings or equipment. Rapid depreciation schedules reward firms that are currently investing heavily in new plant and equipment, but not those who have failed to make such expenditures in the recent past. Faster write-offs provide both funds for more investment and encouragement for such expenditures by offering the opportunity to lower future taxes. The current system of long write-off periods has the opposite effects, and should be abandoned. In order to avoid a sudden (but temporary) drop in tax revenues and an excessively rapid increase in investment, shorter depreciation schedules should be phased in, with the phases coinciding with recessions.

CHANGES IN REGULATORY POLICIES AS INVESTMENT INCENTIVES

It was suggested earlier that the current unstable regulatory climate discourages plant and equipment by making new plants far more expensive and by introducing a larger element of risk as to whether it will be possible to operate new facilities promptly and efficiently when they are scheduled to come on line. This problem could be eased if the various levels of government declared a moratorium on new regulations (except for clear emergencies) and spent the next few years evaluating and simplifying existing restraints. This moratorium would include putting off stiffer regulations in the environmental area which are already written into law and scheduled to go into effect in the next few years. Regulations should not remain in effect merely because they do some "good"; it must be clear that they do *enough* good to justify the costs they impose on an industry and hence on its customers. Regulations should be abandoned that do not meet this criterion.

Delays in gaining regulatory approval for private projects have become another barrier to positive investment decisions. It often takes years to gain approval from a variety of federal, state and local authorities for investment projects that have any significant environmental impact. Even if the facilities are finally determined to meet fully the existing legal requirements, millions of dollars have been spent and years lost without any productive investment having been made. The prospects of such costs and delays often discourage firms from even pursuing profitable opportunities and is particularly inhibiting for small companies which do not have the financial resources to bear the legal costs of the regulatory process. Regulatory authorities should be given a firm deadline (perhaps one year) within which to approve or disapprove proposed projects and explain their decisions. In cases in which regulatory agencies do not reach a defensible conclusion in the required period, approval would be automatic.

Many of the recent problems with regulation have arisen because Congress gave the power to write, interpret and enforce regulations to administrative agencies staffed by people who have little knowledge or interest in economics or economic growth. Many regulators seem to have taken the view that any means is justified by a mandated goal and that the costs of the adopted means are simply irrelevant. During the moratorium on new regulations, employees of regulator agencies might be encouraged to learn the rudiments of economics, with particular emphasis on benefit/cost analysis. Regulatory decisions in Washington or in state capitals should not be made by people who lack an understanding of the concept of costs in addition to an awareness of the goals of the regulatory effort. If the regulatory system were simplified, stabilized and then managed by people who have some knowledge of the realities of economics, a major disincentive for plant and equipment investment in the United States would be removed.

ENERGY POLICY AND INVESTMENT

Since the possibility of another Arab oil embargo, further Iranian (or other) production cutbacks, or additional sharp increases in OPEC prices are clear threats to the U.S. economy, progress toward the goal of sharply reducing U.S. dependence on OPEC oil would considerably improve the U.S. investment climate. As long as the performance of this economy is at the mercy of production decisions made in the Persian Gulf, of unforeseen political instability in oil-exporting countries, and of unpredictable pricing decisions made at OPEC meetings, perceived investment risks will be considerably higher than would otherwise be the case. A combination of increased conservation, attempts to find more oil in non-OPEC countries, and the rapid development of nonoil energy sources is needed, and a continued increase in domestic energy prices is probably the best way to encourage this result. Legal enforcement of domestic energy prices that are well below world levels obviously discourages conservation, new oil discoveries and the development of new energy sources. The case for decontrol of oil and gas prices, perhaps combined with a tax on oil consumption, is compelling. An excise tax on oil consumption would drive consumers away from an energy source that is almost certain to be less readily available in a few decades.[6] Unless there is a large and unforeseen technological breakthrough in the production of alternative energy sources, the United States cannot expect to reduce its reliance on imported oil while abandoning nuclear power. Hence, every feasible attempt must be made to improve the safety of commercial reactors, but construction of new plants and the continued operation of existing facilities are almost a necessity if U.S. dependence on OPEC oil is to be significantly reduced. As soon as it is clear that a program is in place which can reasonably be expected to reduce U.S. vulnerability to OPEC pressures or surprises, the investment climate in the United States will improve considerably.

---

6   The decontrol of domestic oil prices, perhaps combined with a modest "windfall profits tax," could produce some of the desired effects. Domestic prices of oil products would rise sharply, discouraging consumption, and relatively light taxation of newly discovered oil and oil produced through enhanced recovery techniques would maintain incentives for increased production. The complete lack of a tax on windfall profits and its replacement with an excise tax on oil consumption might be preferable but is politically unrealistic. The lack of controls on domestic oil prices and of heavy taxes on increased production should help, and Washington appears to be moving toward that result.

OTHER INVESTMENT POLICY OPTIONS

Direct increases in government investment expenditures on some types of social overhead capital would also be useful in encouraging more rapid economic growth. Much of the U.S. interstate highway system, for example, is now almost two decades old and is in need of renewal. Expenditures to repair, improve and perhaps modestly extend this system could be expected to cut shipping costs in important parts of the economy. Federal programs to encourage rapid renewal of major railroad rights of way would have the same effect. If modest increases in government expenditures on productive social overhead capital can be timed to occur during recessions when resources are readily available, they could provide a significant contribution to the acceleration of economic growth without creating excessive demand pressures throughout the economy.

Finally, it should be noted that because large blocks of resources cannot be expected to move easily or quickly into the production of capital equipment, a sudden or rapid increase in the percentage of GNP being invested in plant and equipment is not realistic. The goal of policy makers should be, instead, to encourage a modest increase in investment during the approaching recession, to be followed by a parallel increase in savings rates as the economy recovers. If as little as 1 extra percent of GNP were shifted from consumption to investment during each year over a period of 5 to 10 years, the long-run impact on the U.S. growth rate would be dramatic, and this could be accomplished without severely disrupting the economy. It will require, however, economic policy making with a long time horizon. Policies cannot be designed with only the next election in mind if such a gradual transformation of the economy is to be arranged. Government planning over the required time period will not be easy for politicians who must face the electorate frequently. It ought to be possible, however, if the goals and advantages of such a long-term policy shift are made clear to the voters.

RESEARCH AND DEVELOPMENT

Research and development is a type of investment, and many of the same factors which would encourage firms to spend more on plant and equipment will also encourage more private R&D. Increased availability of borrowed funds at lower interest rates would help in the financing of research expenditures. A stronger market for newly issued common stocks would help small, high technology firms raise funds for research and innovation purposes. A simplified and more stable regulatory climate would give firms more assurance that newly developed products could be produced and marketed, and would consequently encourage research efforts.

There are some other policy options, however, that could have positive impacts on research efforts. Increased public funding of pure science research in universities and elsewhere would produce more breakthroughs in basic science that provide later opportunities for applications in commercial research. This increase in funding should be carried out slowly and carefully, however, to avoid expenditures on well-meaning but hastily conceived projects on the latest academic fad.

Commercial innovation and research efforts can also be encouraged if the U.S. government is careful not to make any international agreements or understandings which prejudice the legal rights of U.S. inventors. There has been some discussion of shortening the period during which patents are valid as a way to encourage the international flow of technology. Such policy options should be abandoned, and the federal government should instead look for ways to increase the protection that patents provide. Patent protection is a major incentive for inventive activity and, if society wants more inventions, it must not reduce that protection. The federal government should not encourage the transfer of U.S. technology to foreign countries at less than full market prices.

The original Third World demands for technology transfer at the Law of the Seas Conference had to be resisted. If the U.S. government had agreed to require U.S. firms to transfer seabed mining technology to an international agency representing the developing countries at far less than market prices, the interests of American investors would have been severely damaged and research and innovation would have been discouraged elsewhere in the economy. It now appears that these negotiations are moving toward a compromise on the seabed mining question which will impose only moderate costs on the U.S. firms that own the relevant technology and which will allow them to operate profitably. In this and other negotiations with the Third World, it remains important that the U.S. government remember that if the interests of one group of inventors are damaged, research and development is discouraged elsewhere in the economy. Technology is at the core of U.S. comparative advantage in international trade and that comparative advantage should not be given away.

Attitudes toward patents and technology in the antitrust division of the U.S. Department of Justice may be more of a threat to private R&D expenditures than Third World demands. The Department of Justice has required that U.S. firms virtually give away patented technology as part of some antitrust settlements and, if this approach becomes common, it will obviously discourage research efforts by large firms which fear antitrust problems. The obvious purpose of patent laws is to create temporary monopolies as a strong incentive for research efforts, and the goals of these laws should not be compromised or destroyed by excessively aggressive antitrust efforts.

THE TERMS OF TRADE

The effect of worsening international terms of trade on U.S. real incomes is unfortunately a reality about which the government can do little. To the extent that U.S. energy policies here and abroad succeed in reducing the demand for imported oil, the ability of OPEC continually to raise prices will be restrained, which would help. As long as demand for imported oil remains strong, however, one can only expect the OPEC countries repeatedly to push prices up to the detriment of U.S. terms of trade and the real incomes of the American people.

The terms of trade represent another issue in which the demands of the Third World have conflicted with U.S. interests. The "New International Economic Order" agenda included a demand for an international price support program for the major primary products exported by developing countries. The adoption of such a proposal would have cost the OECD countries large sums to finance the support program and would have worsened their terms of trade.

In contrast, programs to stabilize primary product prices around long-term market trends might be made to work to the potential benefit of both producers and consumers. Although the history of such plans is not encouraging, buffer-stock plans might be useful as a means of purchasing and storing primary commodities when prices are below an estimated long-run equilibrium level and for selling these when prices are above that level.[7] If the buffer-stock managers tend to accumulate excessive stocks over a long period, the target price can be lowered and vice versa. The goal of such a program would be to stabilize prices, *not* to push them above long-run market levels. Any realistic approach to such explorations, however, must be based on the lessons of past experience indicating that such commodity stabilization programs are difficult to design appropriately or to operate effectively over extended periods of time.

CONCLUSION

The proposals presented here represent a possible agenda for substantial changes in the structure and direction of U.S. macroeconomic policies. The primary goal is to shift resources out of public and private consumption and into investment in plant and equipment and in research and development. It is not an approach which can be adopted without controversy. Its advantage, however, is that over a period of a few years, the suggested policy shifts could hold great promise for significantly increasing the rate at which the U.S. economy grows, thereby providing greater long-run private consumption possibilities and more tax revenue that can be used to deal with income inequities and other public problems. In the short run, there is a clear conflict between the goals of income redistribution through government intervention and economic efficiency and growth. In the long run, however, there is no such conflict. If the economy can be made to grow considerably faster than it has in recent years, resources will become available to deal with problems of poverty and public needs without discouraging further investment and economic growth. Smaller is not better. More is better. With more output, more income and more tax revenues, the United States can deal adequately with both private and public needs. For these results, however, more economic growth is needed, which will require some temporary compromises in the pursuit of other policy goals.

---

7   The North-South discussions have recently moved away from the concept of international price supports and toward individual commodity buffer stocks which are to be financed in part by a common fund. This is an encouraging development.

National Planning Association

NPA is an independent, private, nonprofit, nonpolitical organization that carries on research and policy formulation in the public interest. NPA was founded during the Great Depression of the 1930s when conflicts among the major economic groups—business, labor, agriculture—threatened to paralyze national decision making on the critical issues confronting American society. It was dedicated to the task of getting these diverse groups to work together to narrow areas of controversy and broaden areas of agreement and to provide on specific problems concrete programs for action planned in the best traditions of a functioning democracy. Such democratic planning, NPA believes, involves the development of effective governmental and private policies and programs not only by official agencies but also through the independent initiative and cooperation of the main private-sector groups concerned. And, to preserve and strengthen American political and economic democracy, the necessary government actions have to be consistent with, and stimulate the support of, a dynamic private sector.

NPA brings together influential and knowledgeable leaders from business, labor, agriculture, and the applied and academic professions to serve on policy committees. These committees identify emerging problems confronting the nation at home and abroad and seek to develop and agree upon policies and programs for coping with them. The research and writing for these committees are provided by NPA's professional staff and, as required, by outside experts.

In addition, NPA's professional staff undertakes research designed to provide data and ideas for policy makers and planners in government and the private sector. These activities include the preparation on a regular basis of economic and demographic projections for the national economy, regions, states, metropolitan areas, and counties; research on national goals and priorities, productivity and economic growth, welfare and dependency problems, employment and manpower needs, energy and environmental questions, and other economic and social problems confronting American society; and analyses and forecasts of changing international realities and their implications for U.S. policies. In developing its staff capabilities, NPA has increasingly emphasized two related qualifications. First is the development of the interdisciplinary knowledge required to understand the complex nature of many real-life problems. Second is the ability to bridge the gap between theoretical or highly technical research and the practical needs of policy makers and planners in government and the private sector.

All NPA reports have been authorized for publication in accordance with procedures laid down by the Board of Trustees. Such action does not imply agreement by NPA board or committee members with all that is contained therein unless such endorsement is specifically stated.

NPA Officers and Board of Trustees

Recent NPA International Publications

Economic Growth Among Industrialized Countries: Why the United States Lags, by Robert M. Dunn, Jr., assisted by Salih N. Neftci (77 pp, May 1980, $5.50), CIR #7, NPA #179.

A Positive Approach to the International Economic Order, Part II: Nontrade Issues, by Alasdair MacBean and V.N. Balasubramanyam (April 1980, $5.00), BN #26, NPA #177.

A Trade Union View of U.S. Manpower Policy, by William W. Winpisinger (52 pp, April 1980, $3.00), BN #27, NPA #176.

The Economic Growth of the United States: Perspective and Prospective, by Solomon Fabricant (95 pp, December 1979, $5.00), CUSP #5, NPA #175.

Canada-U.S. Relations: Policy, Environments, Issues, and Prospects, by Harald von Riekhoff, John H. Sigler and Brian W. Tomlin (150 pp, December 1979, $6.00), CUSP #4, NPA # 173.

A Survey of the Impact of Manufactured Exports from Industrializing Countries in Asia and Latin America: Must Export-Oriented Growth Be Disruptive? by Lawrence G. Franko (56 pp, November 1979, $4.50), CIR #6, NPA #174.

New Patterns of World Mineral Development, by Raymond F. Mikesell (116 pp, September 1979, $5.00), BN #25, NPA #172.

Tales of Two City-States: The Development Progress of Hong Kong and Singapore, by Theodore Geiger and Frances M. Geiger (260 pp, second printing 1979, $7.00), DP #3.

New Investment in Basic Industries, an Occasional Paper prepared by a BNAC Task Force (22 pp, June 1979, $1.00), BN Occasional Paper #1.

U.S. Ownership of Firms in Canada: Issues and Policy Approaches, by Steven Globerman (104 pp, May 1979, $5.00), CUSP #3, NPA #170.

Inflation Is a Social Malady, by Carl E. Beigie (92 pp, March 1979, $4.00), BN #24, NPA #164.

Bilateral Relations in an Uncertain World Context: Canada-U.S. Relations, a Staff Report (111 pp, Nov. 1978, $4.00), CAC #46, NPA #165.

Electricity across the Border: The U.S.-Canadian Experience, by Mark Perlgut (72 pp, Nov. 1978, $4.00), CAC #47, NPA #167.

Research and Development as a Determinant of U.S. International Competitiveness, by Rachel McCulloch (60 pp, Oct. 1978, $3.00), CIR #5, NPA #161.

Welfare and Efficiency: Their Interactions in Western Europe and Implications for International Economic Relations, by Theodore Geiger, assisted by Frances M. Geiger (160 pp, Oct. 1978, $7.00), CIR #4, NPA #160.

The Foreign Trade Practices of Centrally Planned Economies and Their Effects on U.S. International Competitiveness, by Egon Neuberger and Juan Lara (56 pp, Oct. 1977, $3.00), CIR #3, NPA #157.

Also Available from the National Planning Association

NPA Membership is $50.00 per year, tax deductible. In addition to NPA Reports and *New International Realities,* members receive *Looking Ahead & Projection Highlights,* a periodical published four times a year and also available at the separate subscription price of $10.00 (individual copy price is $2.50). NPA members, upon request, may obtain a 30 percent discount on all other additional purchases of NPA publications.

New International Realities, published three times a year, is a periodical written by staff members of NPA's International Division and outside experts. It is available through NPA membership or by separate subscription @$5.00 per year. Individual copy price is $1.75.

A list of publications will be provided upon request. Quantity discounts are given. Please address all orders and inquiries about publications to:

NATIONAL PLANNING ASSOCIATION
Publications Sales Office
1606 New Hampshire Avenue, N.W.
Washington, D.C. 20009
(202) 265-7685

NATIONAL PLANNING ASSOCIATION

1606 New Hampshire Avenue, N.W.
Washington, D.C. 20009

**Economic Growth Among Industrialized Countries:
Why the United States Lags**

CIR Report #7
NPA Report #179

$5.50

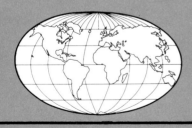

NPA Committee on
Changing International Realities